Educational
Administration

THE LIBRARY OF EDUCATION

A Project of The Center for Applied Research in Education, Inc.

G. R. Gottschalk, Director

Categories of Coverage

I	II	III
Curriculum and Teaching	Administration, Organization, and Finance	Psychology for Educators

IV	V	VI
History, Philosophy, and Social Foundations	Professional Skills	Educational Institutions

Educational Administration

THEODORE J. JENSON

Chairman, Department of Education
Professor of Educational Administration
The Ohio State University

DAVID L. CLARK, 1929-

Associate Dean
College of Education
The Ohio State University

The Center for Applied Research in Education, Inc.
New York

Foreword

Concentrated in the pages of this brief monograph is a panoramic view of the dynamics of educational administration. This overview of the changing scene in the administration of America's schools begins with the legal basis for the organizational structure of our school system and closes with predictions for educational change, program development, and staffing. While the panorama covers the span in time from the origin of our school system to the present, much of the discussion involves changes that have occurred since World War II.

Although the basis for school administration resides in state control and local district operation, there has always been a national interest as well. The authors begin their theme of "dynamic school administration" by illustrating the changing relationships in these three arenas of interest. Chapter II is replete with examples of sociological, cultural, economic, political, and size factors and forces which affect this relationship. The shift from an agrarian to an industrial society, from the rural to the urban way of living, and their consequences for schools, form the setting for changes in school operation.

During the 1950's educational administration came alive. Realizing that change was upon them, school administrators suddenly became alert to the need for coping with change. Not only was it necessary for administrators to change their behavior, but also it was necessary for them to see their tasks in a new light. In Chapter III, the authors portray the struggle of the conscience of administrators as they weigh the various expectations for their role. The authors ask, "Are school administrators policy makers or mere executives of policy?"

This question, and others equally difficult to answer, led administrators to an examination of a number of issues—some in the realm of purpose, others in the art of administration, and still others in what we have come to call the "science of administration." Chapter IV is a progress report on some of the events that have occurred as a result of an attempt to resolve these issues. Although the authors are not satisfied with progress to date, they are encouraged by the application of scientific methods to the study of educational administration. They agree that we are "at a point where a number of provocative theoretical formulations have been made." The payoff, they say, is still to come.

What do we know? Perhaps, it is less than what we once thought we knew. But, say the authors, through the efforts of the Committee for Preparation of Educational Administration, Committee for the Advancement of Educational Administration, University Council on Educational Administration, National Council of Professors of Educational Administration, aided by foundations and research activities sponsored by the Cooperative Research Program and the United States Office of Education, we are learning more about organizational behavior, administrative roles, administrative leadership, the community impact on school administration, and new mechanisms for administrative research.

In looking to the future, the authors see still further acceleration in the rate of change. The effects of change on the nature of education itself, educational program development, and staffing the school to meet new challenges are "precarious" predictions. Will the knowledge "explosion" in educational administration make them any less precarious? The reader is left with this question to ponder.

T. J. Jenson and David L. Clark are keen observers of the educational scene and have contributed in many ways to vanguard movements in educational administration. It is out of their wealth of administrative experience and theoretical investigation that they bring to the profession this clear, concise, and perceptive view of the advancing frontier in educational administration.

JOHN A. RAMSEYER

Educational Administration

Theodore J. Jenson
David L. Clark

Educational Administration presents a broad panoramic yet not superficial view of the entire field of the administration of educational institutions. This is the keystone volume of the Library of Education's series on administration. The volume presents a brief overview of the legal organization of public education, followed by a discussion of the sociological, cultural, economic, political, and size factors which influence this organization. The authors capably present the "agonizing reappraisal" of the role of the administrator that is currently of absorbing interest to scholars in the field, and which centers upon the question, "Are school administrators policy-makers or mere executives of policy?" The discussion of the science of administration which follows is one of the best to be found in the literature. The book closes with an exciting projection of many trends now apparent. No better volume can be recommended to the reader who desires an authoritative description of the present state of knowledge in educational administration.

The authors are well suited to the task of writing this volume. Dr. Jenson is a former superintendent of schools who is now Chairman of the Department of Education and Professor of Educational Administration at Ohio State University. Dr. Clark has had a broad experience in public school administration and in research, having been Director of the Cooperative Research Branch of the United States Office of Education. He is now Associate Dean of the College of Education, Ohio State University. Both have authored several publications.

DANIEL E. GRIFFITHS
Content Editor

Contents

CHAPTER I

Organization and Structure

The central purpose of administration in any enterprise is that of directing and organizing personnel and material resources toward the achievement of its goals and objectives. Educational administration has much in common with other kinds of administration—such as public, governmental, industrial, and business—but it is also unique in some respects, as shall be indicated in this monograph. Its purposes are distinctive, and its sanctions and environment for operations are very different from business and industrial administration.

Since other volumes in this series deal explicitly with educational administrators at various levels and with specific administrative tasks and functions, the content of this presentation has been designed to explore the general phenomenon of administration in public education. While a treatment of a subject such as educational administration in the abstract presents some difficulties for the reader in making direct applications to the concrete and practical, this general overview is designed to provide a basis for a more comprehensive understanding of the operational aspects of administration in education.

The contents of this volume will be presented in the following sequence. First, an overview of the organization and structure under which educational administration operates is presented. Second, the counterpart to the legalistic organization and structure, the situational factors and trends affecting administration, are discussed. Third, the administrative functions, processes, and skills are reviewed. Fourth, theory in educational administration is explored. Fifth, an examination is made of new knowledge and research findings related to educational administration. The sixth and final chapter attempts to take "the look ahead" with projections for the future in educational administration.

1

Organizational Setting

Organization is a function of administration. It is the definition and delineation of the structure of the parts of an enterprise; it is the determiner of practices, jobs, and functions and the systematic arrangement of independent and interdependent parts into a working harmony to accomplish planned purposes.

The basic unit in the organization of public education is the local unit—the school district. While plenary powers are vested in the several states in the management of education, and as long as provisions of the Federal Constitution are not contravened, no state has yet seen fit to operate a wholly state-administered school system. Local school districts, determined by the states, are the vehicles mainly used for the discharge of the state's responsibilities for public education. To these quasi-municipal units the states delegate various kinds and amounts of authority for providing and operating educational programs. Through a long and complex evolution this system of education has developed with a disposition on the part of citizens in local communities to have a definite voice and control in matters pertaining to their schools.

The school district system has experienced and continues to undergo changes, particularly with respect to size and proliferation of districts, but the system persists and is not likely to be abandoned. Educational administration and organization are therefore part of the concept and reality of the school district.

Unique features. Several unique features relating to organization and administration of public education in the United States have been listed by Morphet, Johns, and Reller. A terse resume is listed below:

1. The control of education is relatively decentralized.
2. The people, rather than educators or government officials, are ultimately responsible for the basic policies relating to education.
3. Although primary emphasis is placed on public schools, provisions are also made for private schools.
4. The public schools are safeguarded insofar as possible from partisan political control or influence.
5. Education in the public schools and educational institutions is nonsectarian.
6. Education at public expense is to be available for all in public schools, at least through the secondary grades.

7. Americans believe that those who are responsible for the administration of their schools, as well as those who teach in the schools, should be especially prepared to meet their responsibilities.[1]

Kinds of school districts. Local school districts have only such powers and authority as are granted to them by the states and those "necessarily implied" to make it possible for them to carry out assigned functions. This relationship has been affirmed and well-established by practice, precedent, state constitutional provisions, and court decisions. Thus the administrators and school boards of large urban districts stand in the same over-all relationship to state government as do one-room rural school districts. Unique factors related to local conditions and circumstances have been recognized by special legislation for various kinds of local districts.

Terms relating to the organization of schools, often somewhat confusing to both layman and educators, may be categorized as follows: (1) the common school district, school system, or administrative unit; (2) the neighborhood school center, building or attendance unit; (3) the intermediate district or unit for administration; and (4) the special district.

The school district is a quasi-municipal corporation established and authorized by the state for the local administration and organization of schools. As described by Dawson and others, it is comprised of an area within which a single board or officer has the major responsibility for, and usually considerable autonomy in, the organization and administration of all public education services. It usually has certain powers of taxation for educational purposes that have been delegated by the state.[2]

According to situation and geographic locality, these districts are commonly known by a variety of adjectives, such as common school district, city school district, consolidated school district, central school district, jointures, township district, union free high school district, county unit district, and the like.

The attendance unit, in reality an operational unit, is the area that a building or a set of buildings serves for attendance purposes.

[1] Edgar L. Morphet, Roe L. Johns, and Theodore L. Reller, *Educational Administration—Concepts, Practices, and Issues* (Englewood Cliffs, N.J.: Prentice-Hall, Inc., 1959), p. 5.

[2] Howard Dawson, *et al.*, *Your School District* (Washington, D.C.: Department of Rural Education, National Education Association, 1948), p. 47.

For example, in a city school system these may be characterized by names such as "West High School District" or "Lincoln Elementary School District."

The concept of the intermediate unit stems from the fact that the unit is a combination of local school districts functioning intermediately between the state department of education and the local school districts, providing services for both.

Special districts are areas organized for specific purposes and services, irrespective of other school district organizations in the same area. Examples of these are area vocational and technical schools, community and junior college districts, and special high school districts. These districts usually cut across and bridge existing local district, municipal, and county lines.[3] Except in rare instances, as in some cities with special charters, the state, either directly or by assigned and delegated authority, is responsible for placing or designating all territory within its boundaries into school districts.

Origin and development of school districts. Although there are many similarities between systems of education in the United States, each state's system exhibits unique characteristics. For example, in 1960 Nevada had 17 districts. At the same time there were 40 in Utah, 55 in West Virginia, and 3,800 in Nebraska.[4] While size and population in the states account in part for variance in their systems of education, there are many other factors which have been responsible for differences, including the basic fact that the Federal Constitution is silent on the subject of education, and has, through the Tenth Amendment, "reserved to the states respectively or to the people" all such powers not delegated to the United States by the Constitution or prohibited by it to the states. Hence, the provisions for education are subsumed in the state constitutions, and the organization and structure are delineated accordingly. The federal government has demonstrated interest in education by financing schools under its authority to pursue those activities which contribute to the "general welfare" of the nation. However, it lacks authority to operate the schools of the nation directly.

---

[3] Shirley Cooper and Charles O. Fitzwater, *County School Administration* (New York: Harper & Row, Publishers, 1954), p. 103.

[4] Calvin Grieder, Truman M. Pierce, and William Everett Rosenstengel, *Public School Administration* (New York: The Ronald Press Company, 1961), pp. 8–9.

Many factors other than political and legal ones are credited with influencing the early development of school systems in the states. The first schools in Massachusetts were organized to satisfy religious purposes—the Old Deluder Satan Act of 1642. With the developments that accompanied the close of the Colonial period, cultural determinants had broadened the purposes of education, necessitating the structuring of a common-school system for all where religion was nourished and encouraged in the homes and churches.[5] The need for an educated electorate, the strong urge for local control, the desire for education for all, the belief in the perfectability of man, and an intense conviction that through knowledge and education man increases his power and effectiveness have been cited as other early influences which shaped the course of the educational system.[6] Cubberley cited seven strategic determinants in the struggle for free, tax supported, nonsectarian, state controlled schools:

1. Authorization for the levying of taxes to support education;
2. The elimination of the pauper-school idea, a practice in certain eastern states requiring that parents take paupers' oaths to entitle their children to the advantages of free public education;
3. The establishment of free education for all—free in the sense that schools were operated and supported by taxes rather than by tuition charges, rate-bills, or fees paid by parents;
4. The establishment of state school supervision;
5. The elimination of sectarianism in education;
6. The extension of the common-school idea to include the high school;
7. The establishment of a state university system.[7]

Although situations and factors affecting school districting will be discussed in the next chapter, mention should be made here of some of the pertinent elements affecting district organization. The recent and contemporary factors most frequently mentioned in current literature dealing with school districting are (1) improved highways and transportation facilities, (2) improved communication, (3) expanding demands of the educational program and

[5] R. F. Butts and L. A. Cremin, *A History of Education in American Culture* (New York: Holt, Rinehart & Winston, Inc., 1953), p. 99.
[6] Stephen J. Knezevich, *Administration of Public Education* (New York: Harper & Row, Publishers, 1962), pp. 22–30.
[7] Ellwood P. Cubberley, *The History of Education* (Boston: Houghton Mifflin Company, 1920), pp. 675–708.

school services, (4) costs and economic efficiency factors, (5) new and changing patterns of educational leadership, (6) concerns about the excellence and quality of the school program and services, and (7) court decisions, particularly the decisions of the United States Supreme Court. Although the focus here is upon the public school system, these factors have markedly affected the private and independent schools in their organization.

Organizational Structure in the Local Setting

Under the well-established and long-held principle of strong local control and autonomy at the district level, the voters have become the primary source of authority in the organizational pattern. This concept gives rise to the sentence, "The schools belong to the people." Through powers delegated to them by the state, lay boards of education are elected or appointed as representatives of the citizens in the management function of the local school district. The number of representatives constituting the local board of education varies with statutory provisions in the several states, with as few as three members in some districts and up to fifty or more in some of the "jointure" districts. Usually, however, the school board consists of three, five, seven, eleven, or such relatively small numbers organized with stipulated officers and legally defined duties and responsibilities. These legislative groups are usually known as the board of trustees, the board of school trustees, the board of education, or simply the school board.

Duties of the board. In spite of the sometimes popular notion that the schools are run and governed by the superintendent and his staff, and that the authority of the board of education is a "paper" or "legalistic" matter, the realities of the power and control of the board should not be underestimated.

The legal status of the board of education is that of an agent of the state with prescribed authority and responsibility to execute the state's function of education at the local level. The functions of the board are threefold: (1) policy making, (2) legislative, and (3) evaluative. The board of education is a creature of the legislature and exercises those powers delegated by the legislature. It is responsible for the operational organization of the school system and thereby assumes such duties as (1) general personnel management—hiring and firing employees; (2) determining program and services; (3) financial management; (4) management of buildings and facilities; (5) representing the voters in the district; and (6) representing the state in its educational function at the local level.

The local school executive. Practically, a lay board must employ technical and professional assistance in the execution of its functions. Thus the continuum of the organizational structure is extended—citizens, board of education, and an administrator commonly known as the superintendent of schools. He is responsible for administering the schools under the board of education. In a similar manner, he, with the board, employs administrative assistants, principals, teachers, special service personnel, and others to operate the school program. Thus the authority levels in a local school system, described by Griffiths, Clark, and others as a "tall organization," may be diagramed as in Figure 1.[8]

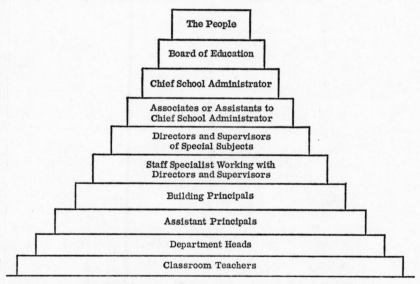

Figure 1. Example of Tall Organization of a School System.

It may be noted that there are ten authority levels depicted in Figure 1; that is, there are nine authority levels between the teacher

[8] Daniel Griffiths, David L. Clark, D. Richard Wynn, and Laurence Iannaccone, *Organizing Schools for Effective Education* (Danville, Ill.: The Interstate Printers and Publishers, Inc., 1962), p. 21.

and the public being served. Figure 2 shows diagrammatically the relationships of authority levels in a "flat" organization.[9] In this organizational structure there are only four authority levels between the teacher and the people, and only one level between the teacher and the chief school administrator. The illustrations shown here are symbolic of the unitary line and staff organization. Practical organizational charts of either the flat or the tall organization may be far more definitive and complex depending upon the size of the operation.

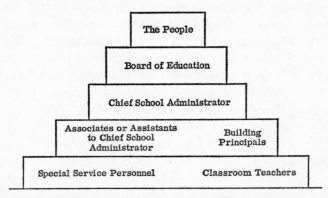

Figure 2. A Diagrammatic Example of Flat Organization.

The pattern of organization must in a large degree be determined by the purposes of the organization, size, philosophy of administration, and important factors in the local situation. In the interest of better communication, authorities seem to agree that the flatter the organization the better. The span of control for the chief administrator and others, however, must be kept within manageable limits.

The County and Intermediate District

Our county unit of government evolved from the English model. England provided for local geographic areas, counties, and Earldoms, which were deemed the smallest geographic units eligible to present petitions to the Crown and for which there was established a sheriff. As in our system, the county served as a bridge between the local and the state government. The social origins

---

[9] *Ibid.*, p. 22.

of the bases for the proliferation of counties in the various states is somewhat obscure. One basis for determining the number and size is said to have been the convenience factor in the distance necessary to travel to hold meetings of the county commissioners. Another strong factor influencing the formation of counties was the determined desire to keep as much local control as possible. Thus the units of government that have been firmly established are the town, village, city, county, and state, each with a well-defined relationship to organization and administration of education.

The earliest administrative controls in counties were largely inspectorial in nature and were handled by various designated county government officials. In 1829, Delaware established the first county superintendent whose sole duties were supervision and visitation of schools. New York followed Delaware's example in 1843, and by 1879 twenty-eight states had established the county superintendency. County superintendents have been usually appointed by the county boards except in states where they are elected by the people.

Evolution and change in the concepts of the duties and functions of the county superintendent's office, the inception of regional and intermediate units in several states, and the development of county school districts in some states have created a situation in which no nationally uniform pattern of county organization for educational administration exists. One element common in the structures of all plans, however, provides that the county unit act in a liaison and intermediary capacity between the strictly local school organization and the state. Among the chief functions provided are supervision, special services, record keeping, certification, distribution of aids and apportionments, in-service education for teachers, recruitment, and the like. The county superintendent, in addition to his enforcement and liaison responsibilities, has been assumed to be an educational leader, particularly for rural education. Even in situations where urban districts have been exempted from county or intermediate district controls, the county office serves as a mediating agency in many matters.

State Educational Organization and Administration

The state has a strategic and significant position in the organizational structure for the education of American youth. Vested with plenary powers in matters of education by the Federal Constitution, each state has made provisions in its constitution for organizing and operating a system of education for the people within its boundaries. Although the local district is commonly thought of as having full authority and responsibility for education, actually it has only such powers and rights as have been delegated to it by the state legislature; it functions as an agency of the state. In this respect, the local school district is different from other local units of government such as villages, cities, townships, and the like. Public education, at all levels, operates within the framework of being an arm of the state. Thus the significance of the state in the framework of organization and structure for education is solidly established.

This recognition of the responsibility of all the people in the state for the development and execution of the state's function in education developed slowly and along many divergent lines. Having no pattern to follow, and with only the mandate of responsibility, each state has developed its own system, copying the best and most applicable elements of the systems developed in older states.

The development of state systems of education. The slow and uneven development of state educational systems may be traced to (1) early patterns and commitments before the nation was organized; (2) the effects of ordinances such as those of 1785 and 1787 related to western portions of the nation prior to statehood; and (3) the early establishment of a commitment to fiscal policies, especially as related to financing and the use of public funds and resources exclusively for public education. The prototype of the state board of education was established in New York in 1784 with limited responsibilities for colleges and academies. The first state board of education with responsibilities for a comprehensive system of schools for the state was established in Massachusetts in 1837. By 1870, most states had established state boards and/or systems of state organization for education.

Chief state school officers. With the development of state systems for education and state boards of education came the need for state school administrators, generally known as superintendents of public instruction or chief state school officers. This office, like other aspects of the development, evolved by stages, with many of the earlier state superintendents designated as *ex officio* while serving in other official state capacities. The expansion and growth of state school organizations has, of course, long since required the full-time efforts of competent state school administrators in all states. The patterns of elections and appointments, however, still vary from state to state. Terms of office range from two years to indefinite tenure serving "at the will and pleasure of the state board." Elections to the office in many states are on either a partisan or nonpartisan basis, with the entire electorate having a voice in the selection at the polls; in other situations, the state board selects and appoints.[10]

The state board of education.   With the exception of Hawaii and Alaska—still in the process of making firm their state organizations for education—and of Illinois, Michigan, and Wisconsin, all states have a state board responsible for major aspects of the public school program. The proliferation of state boards for various educational programs and functions has been phenomenal. The Beach and Will study (see footnote 10) indicated 231 state boards of education for various purposes in the then 48 states. Vocational education, higher education, colleges and universities, and state residential schools for blind, deaf, and handicapped persons are among the separate educational functions for which state boards have been constituted. Thus, with few exceptions, most states have one or more "state boards" for education. The functions, duties, and powers of these boards range from advisory to policy-making and regulatory activities, depending on the powers vested in them by statutes.

The state department of education.   The development of a state organization for education brought with it an administrative unit commonly referred to as the "state department of education" or the "state department of public instruction," which includes the state superintendent and a staff of professional and nonprofessional workers to administer the duties of the office. In 1940 there were 3,718 persons employed on state department staffs, and it is estimated that this number approached 20,000 in 1960.

Leadership, coordination, supervision, inspection, enforcement, research, consultation, allocation of appropriations, certification of teachers and other workers, and planning and service functions are

---

[10] Ford F. Beach and Robert F. Will, *The State and Education,* Miscellaneous No. 23 (Washington, D.C.: Government Printing Office, 1955), pp. 11–30.

among the contributions made to education in the states by the state department staffs. In addition, the state departments serve as liaison agents between in-state and out-of-state organizations and agencies having a relation to educational enterprises within the state.

Federal Educational Organization and Administration

Although the Federal Constitution is silent on matters of public education and ostensibly reserved these obligations and responsibilities for the individual states in the union, any student of organization and structure in modern education cannot overlook the impact of the federal government in matters relating to the education of the youth of the country. Its influence has been pervasive and highly significant. For a detailed description of the functioning of the federal government in education the reader is referred to the Library of Education volume by Pierce, *Federal, State, and Local Government in Education.*

Summary

This overview of the general organization and structure of educational administration began with the description of the local administrative unit, the school district, and with the focus on the local unit. It showed the relationships that exist between the local unit and the county, intermediate district, and state and federal organizations for educational administration. The origin and development of school districts in the states, with varying patterns and designators, result in what amounts to fifty systems of education. Except in the new states of Alaska and Hawaii where constitutional provisions for education are yet to be finalized, the one common element in all states is the focus on the identification of the school district with a definite localized area.

The internal administrative organization of the local district, including the lines of authority and the conventional organization patterns for staffing local units, have been described in a general way. It has been indicated that education is a function of the state and that the state alone has general plenary powers in all matters related to education. All other agencies work through and with the state in its functions of providing education at the local level.

Through the contents of this chapter an effort has been made to review the formal and structured administrative and organizational settings and relationships of local school districts. Situational factors relating to the setting for local district operation will be discussed in the next chapter.

CHAPTER II

Situational Factors

The counterpart of the formal and legalistic organization and structure discussed previously is the impact of situational factors surrounding the locus of operations. Regardless of its structured setting, administration in any local situation is affected by circumstances and trends, many of which have significant conditioning dimensions. This is particularly true in educational administration. Among the most telling factors are those related to social, economic, political, size, and psychological phenomena. These, in many ways, are quite as important to an understanding of the local setting for administration as those factors which stem from legal aspects and relationships.

The Centerville Case

Situational changes and developments are key elements in the story of Centerville—conditions and circumstances common to many, if not most, communities. In a ten-year period Centerville was almost completely transformed from a small, self-contained, and independent city community located on a major highway twenty-five miles outside of Metro to an urban community with the complexity of a major metropolitan area. Situational factors changed so rapidly that educational and civil administrations experienced serious difficulties in keeping up with changes. Problems were met as they arose, and there was little or no time for advanced planning in most instances. Some highlights of the situational factors in Centerville follow.

What were the factors that shaped situations in Centerville? Many of them were sociological in nature, dealing with human association and its development, forms, and functions. These factors included intensified urbanization, population expansion, social forces, pressures from groups in the community, symbiotic relationships of groups, and citizen participation in the affairs of government and education. Other factors centered on economics: new and

14

increasing expenditure levels to meet new demands, competition for revenues, controls and limitation in financing, and concerns over economic efficiency. Other factors were political in nature and involved the science of government and controls, municipal and governmental unit relationships, boundary line problems, and the school district relationships with local, county, and state units of government. Still other factors were largely related to size: bigness of operation, the psychological effects of communication problems, and the impersonalness that comes with large operations.

Over the years, Centerville had been slowly drawn into the orbit of the major metropolitan area. More and more people lived in Centerville and worked in Metro. The twenty-five miles that separated the two cities had developed into a "strip-city" with homes and small business establishments along the entire route. The small city had been changing slowly in character, but about eight years ago changes began to occur more rapidly. A 500 unit high-level subdivision known as Cloverdale Estates was approved for Centerville's north side. Streets and water and sewer facilities were extended. Zoning had to be reexamined to assure sustained quality in the new subdivision, and after some difficulties new zoning ordinances were established. Ranch and split-level homes were built, sold, and occupied at an unbelievable pace. The newcomers were largely from the executive and management class. Many of them, having been transferred from other parts of the nation, came from former suburban homes. They brought their values with them.

Immediately, the schools and the city began to feel the pressure from the new residents: Why don't we have a junior high school? When can we get a kindergarten started? What plans are there for a new school nearer Cloverdale Estates? Why are classrooms so crowded? How can Cloverdale get representation on the school board and on the city council? Why are property taxes so high? Why are the new residents not received with a better reception in local churches and in social and civic organizations?

These were some of the many concerns from the Cloverdaleites, but the old residents of Centerville had concerns too. They saw the new residents as "foreigners" invading the sanctum of long-established ways and practices in Centerville. But this was just the beginning of what was to come for Centerville.

Five years ago a site was selected for a huge defense installation, straddling the south city limits of Centerville. The next two years saw the city mushroom with developments of all kinds. The population doubled, tripled, and continued to increase. School housing could not keep up with the need, even though every effort had been made to stay abreast of growth developments. The new workers in the community came from everywhere. Property values skyrocketed. In fact, almost everything in Centerville was either engulfed or changed, and at a devastating pace. The long-time, stable board of education was replaced with new members. The new residents dominated the city council. The old power structure in Centerville had been replaced with new and multiple power structures. The old intimacy in the community had been replaced by the cool strangeness that comes with bigness.

In ten years Centerville has been completely transformed, and although as a case in point it is an extreme example, it serves to illustrate the impact of situational factors. Every community is characterized by situations and circumstances that have a definite bearing and impact on the setting for educational administration.

Sociological Factors

Human association and its development, forms, and functions have a definite influence on situational factors that affect educational administration in a community. Some of the more prominent manifestations of these sociological factors include urbanization, population shifts and changes, social forces, pressures, symbiotic group relationships, and various forms of lay participation in school and community enterprises. All these elements are potential sources of problems to school administration.

Urbanization. In everyday terms, urbanization is the process by which communities tend to become like cities, to have population concentration. The trend toward urbanization is a nationwide phenomenon due in part to (1) increasing population, (2) job opportunities resulting from industrialization, and (3) the desires of people for the services, conveniences, and benefits that come with urban living. It is a well-known fact that when people contemplate relocation, they are concerned about job opportunities, schools, churches, and transportation. The impact upon schools and education is obvious. School housing must be expanded to meet increasing numbers. The school program must be adjusted to meet new and more widely divergent needs. New projections and planning for the future become standard practice.

Although not interdependent with urbanization, the mobility of population results in problems for the urban school system. Stories of students having attended several urban school systems in a single academic year are not myths. How do students adjust in these situations? How does the school adjust to these "in-and-outers"? A study for the year 1956–57 showed that 31,834,000 of the civilian population over age one changed residence within the year.[1] It is safe to say that the brunt of this shift and change was borne by urban school administrations.

Population. So much has been written about increasing populations and the impact of numbers that only minimal attention is given to it here. While there is no intent to minimize the problems resulting from magnitude of population, numbers of students to be educated, schoolbuilding construction to house them, teachers needed to instruct the burgeoning numbers, and the like, this is but one aspect of the total problem related to population.

The increasing population is not merely one to which simple arithmetic progression can be applied; it has geometric progression propensities. Although any current head-count of persons to be served creates certain problems for schools and the school administration, it is what comes next that provides a basis for concern. Each new census of population brings the possibilities for more family units—that is, more people at each age level. Couple this with the factor of increasing longevity and it becomes clear that more and more demands will be made on community resources.

The implications for educational administration of problems related to population includes not only those mentioned before, but also potentially new concerns: competition for revenues, maintaining good public relations with the segment of the population not connected with the schools, obtaining favorable votes on bond issues, communication problems, and maintaining standards of excellence and quality in education.

Special problems. Educational administration faces many spe-

---

[1] Bureau of the Census, U.S. Department of Commerce, *Mobility of Population of the United States, April 1956 to 1957,* Current Population Reports, Series P–20, No. 82 (Washington, D.C.: The Bureau, July 21, 1958), Table 2, p. 9.

cial problems arising from the characteristics and concentration of population. The problems of the "core city" are a good example. In all major cities the schools face the problem of dealing with and providing for a concentration of "disadvantaged" to be educated. Where are the teachers trained to handle the disadvantaged to be found? How does a city system organize to meet the needs of these youngsters? What special assistance is needed to help cities meet these problems? Is new legislation needed?

In many of our major cities urban renewal projects pose new and vexing problems to the school administration. For the most part, these projects are in older sections of the city where the school facilities have been outmoded and in some cases abandoned. What does the school system do in cases of this kind? In massive redevelopment projects, such as the south side in Chicago, new school complexes have been established, but what can be done where the development is too large to be ignored but not large enough to merit special facilities? Problems like this call for new and imaginative solutions.

It is generally agreed among political scientists that the "heart areas" of our major metropolitan complexes are in serious trouble. Much of the better leadership has moved out to the suburbs. The new leadership is both untested and inexperienced. Property values have depreciated through aging and obsolescence. Serious imbalances are created in the support of and execution of municipal services and educational obligations. These and other problems, such as traffic, parking, welfare and the like, cannot be ignored by the educational administration in large cities.

Social forces and pressures. Educational administration is subject to social forces and pressures in every community. In the Centerville case the pressure was applied for junior high schools, for representation on the school board and the city council, for more language instruction, for new schools in certain areas, and so forth. These forces and pressures cannot be dismissed (for long, at least) by the school administration.

The implications for educational administration of these forces and pressures are legion. Since they cannot be ignored, a system must be implemented for (1) detection and identification, (2) weighing and evaluating, (3) determining courses of action, and

(4) implementing, coordinating, and appraising the actions to be used.

Symbiotic relationships and lay participation. Social symbiosis, as used here, refers to the association of dissimilar groups existing together in harmony and for each other's mutual benefit. It also refers to social systems, boards, commissions, interest groups, and the like that must work together in the community. For example, an elementary school district in Illinois could be associated with and be a part of a township high school district, a municipal subdivision, a county, a sanitary district, or a conservation district —all structured social systems with which it must live and share mutual benefits. These are external symbiotic groups.

Similarly, school districts have internal symbiotic group relationships. Examples are the school board, advisory councils, parent groups, staff groups, and student groups. All exist as more or less separate entities, but each needs the other to accomplish common purposes and objectives. The fact of symbiotic relationships cannot be denied, but it is the nature of the relationship that concerns educational administration. How do groups work together for common purposes? What are the obligations of the school administration in fostering better symbiotic relationships? What is the school administrator's role in this regard?

There are also many lay groups and unofficial agencies that seek a relationship and identification with the schools in a community. Seldom, if ever, in the history of education in the United States has there been a greater interest in education and schools on the part of laymen. Beginning roughly with World War II, the mounting problems of education began to command the attention of citizens and lay groups. Although civic groups, women's clubs, service groups, and the like have always had an interest in education and youth, the interest was intensified during the war period. Stories about the plight of education became newsworthy; magazine articles paraded the good and bad aspects of education; alarmists sounded cautions; a succession of books, written mainly by noneducators, about education began to hit the market; radio and television media scheduled time for concerns about education; and, in general, the lay consciousness about education was developed and intensified.

With full recognition of the many values of this intensified interest in education on the part of the layman, unofficial agencies, and pressure groups, the phenomenon has become an integral part of the setting in which educational administration functions. It is noteworthy that most of these groups have a sincerity of purpose in what each thinks will cause improvements in the educational system. They also serve as communication media, influence individual interests, opinions, and values, and function as a mechanism for crystallizing and implementing patterns of action. It is a mark of insight and wisdom on the part of an administration that works effectively with lay groups.

Propelled by the emerging culture of the past two decades, minority groups in most communities have taken on a much higher visibility than they formerly did. New laws, legal interpretations, and decisions, as well as new enforcement standards, have given a new significance to the opinions and voices of minority groups in local civic and educational affairs. Dahlke puts it bluntly in saying that the schools are surrounded by a ring of special interest groups which are watching, criticizing, and trying to exert their influence to see their own values realized.[2] Each group wants its own orthodoxy in the schools.

Another intriguing aspect of the operations of many unofficial agencies comes through what Loomis and Beegle have called the "third house" operations—lobbying.[3] A glance at the registered lobby lists in most states verifies their conclusion. Many of the lobbies are not interested as much with education directly as with certain other elements such as taxes or the promotion of causes— conservation, safety, value of dairy products, citizenship, and the like for which they seek legislative support with indirect or direct relatedness to the schools and education. Promotion and lobbying activities are not restricted to the legislative halls, they also operate at the school board level, in the P.T.A., the school administration, and wherever an impact can be made. The point here is not to make a value judgment of lay groups, unofficial agencies, and pressures, but rather to recognize them as a phenomenon that must be dealt with in administration.

Citizen participation and involvement in the administration of

[2] H. Otto Dahlke, *Values in Culture and Classroom* (New York: Harper & Row, Publishers, 1958), p. 63.

[3] Charles P. Loomis and J. Allan Beegle, *Rural Social Systems* (Englewood Cliffs, N.J.: Prentice-Hall, Inc., 1950), p. 611.

the educational enterprise in the community is fast becoming the rule rather than the exception. The school administration which frowns on Study Councils, Citizen Committees, Advisory Committees, Citizens' Councils, Parent Organizations, Booster Groups, and the like is out of touch with reality, if not naïve with respect to the trends. The feeling that lay groups could benefit education became so widespread a few years ago that in 1949 the National Citizens Commission for the Public Schools was organized with the avowed purpose to stimulate public interest in education and to develop local study and action groups. In 1956 the Commission was reorganized into the National Citizens Council for Better Schools.[4] By 1958 some 12,000 citizens' committees had been organized in local communities across the nation. Much of significant value to education has been accomplished through the efforts of these groups.

The important and somewhat unique significance of the participation in educational administration may be summed up by stating that: (1) lay groups and unofficial agencies in the community are manifesting a definite interest in education; (2) most of these interests are value oriented toward what the groups or organizations feel are for the betterment or preservation of educational values, community welfare, economic efficiency, and progress; and (3) educational administration is obliged to learn to live with and operate effectively with increasing involvement of citizens in school affairs. Increasingly, in the complexities of society and the corresponding competition for commitments of citizens for worthy causes, educational administration must be concerned with every means possible to assure a solid commitment on the part of the people in the community for quality education and excellence in the schools.

Economic Factors

The setting for educational administration is constantly influenced by factors related to economics. What happens to the economic structure of the community when the main industry closes and dismisses its workers? What is the impact of a new industry such as that illustrated in the Centerville case? What problems arise resulting from increased costs? How does educational administration

---

[4] National Citizens Council for Better Schools, 9 East 40th Street, New York 16, N.Y.

cope with the problem of excessive program demands that are un-realistic in relation to the community's ability to finance them? What are the stewardship responsibilities of educational administration?

The foregoing questions and others of a similar nature seem to point to several concerns for educational administration: (1) the impact of new and increased expenditure for education; (2) controls and limitations on finance for education; (3) competition for revenues and support; and (4) the need for depth considerations of ways and means for more efficient operation while maintaining quality and excellence.

Educational costs. Expenditures for education have risen sharply in recent years. In the decade 1951–61, based on 1959 consumer price levels, the increase averaged better than ten per cent per year. Even when some of the backlog factors are minimized —such as the need for new buildings, needed increases in teachers' salaries to update and effect a better alignment of wages for school employees with other employees in the community, and the like— educational costs have increased substantially. Predictions are hazardous, but best estimates seem to indicate that current outlays for elementary education, attributable to increased eligible school-age population alone, will increase by another fifteen per cent by 1970; for secondary education, estimates of increased outlays for the same reason range from thirty-five to fifty per cent.

Based on figures for 1962, it has been estimated that the current expense per year per pupil approximates $400. One projection is that this figure will rise to $720 by 1970, based upon current price indexes and minimum standards of quality.[5]

Other pertinent factors that will influence expenditure levels include (1) increasing numbers to be educated; (2) more students continuing in school longer; (3) better professionally trained staffs; (4) a greater per cent of men and career teachers and correspondingly fewer women teachers leaving the profession for marriage, homemaking, and raising families; (5) higher salary levels; and (6) more fringe benefits for employees. Price levels, inflation, general wage levels and the over-all economy will most certainly be reflected in expenditure trends and levels for education. In addition, the

---

[5] "National Education Association Research Bulletin," Vol. 40, No. 4 (Washington, D.C.: The Association, 1962), p. 99.

growing demand for improved quality and excellence in education is likely to cost more.

The implications for educational administration of new and increased expenditure levels are obvious; more thorough justifications for revenue requests will be expected, and the "watch-dogs" of the budget will insist on the best possible efficiency in operations. Administration will be looked to for new and imaginative ways of providing quality education in the most economical and efficient manner possible.

Competition for revenues. Educational administration faces increasing competition for financial support. The competition comes from many sources. A portion of the demand for new revenues comes from local sources—requests for more and improved municipal services, better streets, more recreational facilities, more health and library services, better fire protection, and the like. At the same time, the county and state units of government are called upon to upgrade, improve, and institute new services, all of which need funding. In a similar manner the federal government exacts its requirements for its many and varied needs. All the demands descend upon the taxpayer.

In some states and local situations the burden on property taxation has nearly reached the breaking point. Operating levies and bond issues have encountered serious difficulties at the polls. The voter is caught in the middle, and he is unable to do much about it for two reasons: first, he feels that he is quite remote from the decision making involved in many of the taxes imposed upon him; second, there is a certain inevitability about the tax drain for defense, security, social security, and other established program needs.

The whole matter of tax structures, inequities, and revenue producing sources is being studied at all levels. Educational administration must share in this process with positive approaches to the problems, rather than merely defending its need for a share of the tax take.

Political Factors

School administration is inherently identified with the science of government. The school district is a quasi-municipal corporation and assumes a posture under law in many aspects similar to that of other units of government. The school district is irrevocably tied to significant relationships with other units of government—the city, the township, the county, and the state. The same clientele is involved; the support comes from the same *sources;* and, as with other units of government, the objectives of the school district are to provide desired services to the people in the community. In this relationship the school administrator needs to see himself as a member of a public administration team in the community. Therefore, such aspects of political factors as municipal relationships, fiscal relations, boundary factors, and involvement of educational administration with other governmental agencies and units seem pertinent to this discussion.

Municipal relationships. The relationships of educational administration with municipal units may be roughly categorized as internal and external. The internal relationships are those with municipal units of which the school district is an integral part; the external relationships are those with neighboring municipalities and governmental units. A city school district has internal relationships with the city government in the city of which it is a part, but it also has relations with suburbs, adjacent townships, and neighboring cities. There is also a high possibility that it has relationships with other school districts in joint operations, provisions for special educational facilities, tuition, transportation, interscholastic activities, and the like. The suburban and country school districts are similarly situated, and their relationships to other municipalities may be even more complex. The matter of annexation of territory to parent cities, for example, could be explored for its impact on municipal relationships. Experience has shown that annexation of territory has provided some of the most difficult problems of school administration-municipal relationships.

A brief review of some of the internal issues faced by school administration and municipal administration may serve to exemplify the need for mutual good relations. Such common issues of public policy as population increase, inflation, race relations, allocation of resources, and relations of local units to federal and state governments are common concerns of both municipal and educational administration. With some exceptions, school administration has stood aloof from such problems, with the view that they are mainly concerns of the municipal government. There are, however, excellent examples of where the school and municipal relations have been of the nature and quality to cope with mutual concerns very successfully. This view should be the rule rather than the exception.

Fiscal relations with municipalities. Although fiscal relations between school districts and municipalities are usually delineated in state statutes, the degree of autonomy of the school district in a community is an important aspect of the setting for school administration. While this relatedness usually refers to fiscal matters—fiscal dependence or independence—having to do with budget approval from some other governmental unit, in some instances it also includes other actions of the school district. Other instances of dependence—that is, where the school district's actions are subject to approval and review by another governmental unit or agency—include encumbrance of funds, acquisition of property, interpretations and definitions made by noneducational agencies, audit findings, and the like.

The legality of fiscal dependence for school districts has been questioned in several states on the grounds that since education is a state function and school board members are actually state officers, their actions should not be subject to review by an agency of less status and authority. The point has been firmly established that any reviewing agency may exercise only that power with which it is specifically endowed by the statutes.

It would appear, however, that regardless of the fiscal independence of the school district, the school administration has an obligation to work closely with other governmental units and agencies in matters of finance. Coordination and planning of fiscal affairs should be a concern of all agencies serving the community. Regardless of authority or legal status, cooperation between school and municipal administrations is desirable.

Boundary lines. It would be difficult to explain to the parent of a kindergarten child living on the south side of 36th Street, for example, why her child may not attend the school a block away to the north but must attend another school five blocks to the south, simply because the child lives in a certain school district bounded on the north by a mythical line down the center of 36th Street. Nevertheless, these are the facts of life in school administration; where there are boundary lines, inevitably people will live near or on them. There are instances on record where children have attended the "wrong" school for their entire education, unaware that their residence was just outside the school district.

Boundary lines are necessary to delineate and circumscribe attendance areas, administrative units, municipalities, and political subdivisions. Once established, they have a tendency to become fixed and permanent. In fact, many of these boundaries were established years ago under very different circumstances of travel and communication. Take the matter of counties in states: one wonders whether a given small state would be divided into 88 counties if the determination were to be made today.

School-district lines have come under sharp scrutiny in recent years, particularly in school-district reorganization ventures. This is not to imply that all boundary lines do not serve a purpose or should be abolished. Some boundaries, however, which have outlived their usefulness deserve to be reexamined. In any event, boundary lines are a matter of special importance in the setting for school administration.

Involvement. Probably no other governmental administrative unit has as wide direct and indirect involvement with other governmental units and agencies as does the school district. Yet paradoxically, as pointed out by U.S. Commissioner of Education Keppel, school administration has looked upon its job as "the improvement of the quality of what is taught and the effectiveness of teaching in the schools. Anything else is a diversion and a mistake."[6] The tendency has been for school administration to take for granted that education (the school) is a thing apart, to be detached from the issues of the day as far as possible. Perhaps for this reason school administration has tended to feel that the only aspects of public policy and major involvements with other governmental agencies and units that fall within its range are those related to allocation of funds, services, and resources for the school and education.

None can say that obtaining funds is not important. The community expects the school administration to go after its legitimate share of funds, equipment, and services from all sources available to it. But this is a one-way involvement, sometimes almost apologetic, since the school administration has made little or no contribution to the public-policy decisions which made the resources

---

[6] Francis Keppel, *Public Policy and School Administration* (Cambridge, Mass.: New School Development Council, 1961), p. 14.

available. The administrator, in a vain effort to "keep above politics," has blocked a legitimate execution of a responsibility.

Careful analysis of the involvement of administration in decision-making and policy development relating to the general issues of the community suggests that there is room for a sane, sagacious, and prudent exploration of its possibilities. This theory, as suggested by Riemers, might be found to be a prudent guide to grappling with real problems of life and the practical science of government.[7] A better relationship must be encouraged between school administration and the various other administrations concerned with the problems, issues, and well-being of the community.

Size Factors

The factors of size play an important role in the setting for educational administration. There are concerns about the size of classes, rooms, attendance areas, administrative units, laboratory areas, playgrounds, gymnasiums, recreation facilities, and so forth. The trend, with the possible exception of class size, has been toward larger units, space requirements, and facilities. Even the revered notion of small classes has yielded to combinations for large group instruction where practicable. As an example, the increase in square footage standards per pupil station in New York in 1954 over 1940 standards illustrates the point (see Table 1).

TABLE 1[8]

SQUARE FOOTAGE STANDARDS PER PUPIL STATION
IN SCHOOL BUILDINGS

	1940	1954	Increase
Elementary Classroom	16.5 sq. ft.	28.5 sq. ft.	73%
Kindergarten	25	35	40
General Shop	50	75	50
Music, Art or Drawing	16.5	25	52

Space allotment per pupil is a much debated question, especially in view of the fact that practice indicates widely divergent ratios in

---

[7] Neal Riemer, "The Revival of Democratic Theory in the United States," *The Annals,* November, 1962, p. 35.

[8] Temporary Commission on Educational Finances, Final Report, *Financing Public Education in New York State* (Albany, N.Y., 1956), p. 318.

space provisions for ostensibly the same program use. Educational administration is constantly faced with the questions of size relationships. Some findings, many of which are based upon opinions and limited documentary evidence, seem to indicate (1) that extremes in minimum size are uneconomical, inefficient, and do not foster effective educational programs; and (2) that maximums in size do not necessarily guarantee economic efficiency and effective educational programs. There is good evidence that units which are too small are economically inefficient and very limiting in terms of program possibilities; it also indicates that beyond certain sizes both economic and program efficiencies appear to plateau.

Administrative units. In the local setting, administration is faced first with the question of size of the administrative units which can be operated economically, efficiently, and effectively. Much literature has been produced on the size of an optimum administrative unit, particularly in the publications and studies on reorganization of school districts. The most frequently mentioned characteristics of satisfactory, effective, and ideal districts are (1) large enough child population for good educational services for at least grades 1–12; (2) conformation with "natural sociological areas"; (3) satisfactory distance factors for walking or bus travel; and (4) adequate financial base for supporting an effective educational program.

Obviously there is no pat answer to how big an administrative unit should be. More specifically, the problem ultimately comes down to the questions of "how big" or "how big for what." Research on this topic is most inadequate. The bind comes in situations where the administration finds the district too small to do what it would like to do, or not quite large enough to provide on its own some of the services and needs in the local schools. Confederations, cooperative efforts with adjacent school districts, and the initiation of intermediate coordinating and service districts are being explored in many situations as possible partial solutions to size problems.

Educational program. Most important in any consideration of size is its program impact. Most opinions on secondary school enrollments advocate at least 300–500 students on the theory that even the senior class might have upwards of 50 to 100 students. This would make possible adequate members to offer a rich and varied program to meet the widely divergent needs of youth, with an assurance that classes and sections would have sufficient enrollment to operate effectively, efficiently, and economically. It is hardly feasible to offer a very rich program to a high school senior class of 15–20 students.

The concern about size in relation to program offerings is obvious, but it is of little comfort to an administration faced with very small enrollments and a desire to offer a full and rich program. The ingenuity and imagination in solving these problems by some school systems are most commendable. Experiments in small school cooperation, such as that in New York State, sponsored by the Ford Foundation and others appear to hold much promise.[9]

Centralization. It is wishful thinking to imagine that reorganization and centralization, as a means to achieve desired size units, are the solutions to all problems. Large size brings with it many problems and generates still more operational concerns. A common concern related to "bigness" is psychological in origin—a general aversion to anything big as something cold, threatening, burdened with red tape, impersonal, unsympathetic to individual concerns and needs, fettered with communication problems, inflexible, and over-concentration of power in a few individuals who are unable to keep in touch with local concerns and opinions and who are prone to possible wastes, oversights, and built-in inefficiencies. Of course, these deficiencies are purposely overdrawn here, but there is enough reality in the aversion to make it a factor of contention.

An often suggested remedy for all the ills of centralization and bigness is expressed in the phrase "split-it-up"—effect a dual or multiple organizational schemata, one for business affairs, one for instruction, one for plant and facilities, and so on. While this remedy appears to have possibilities, there is some evidence to indicate that it only compounds the problems and clearly indicates the superiority of the unit plan of organization.[10]

Other research findings on the problems of centralization and central office operations point to the fact that administration must redefine its role in a large organization to cope with problems of

---

[9] *Catskill Area Project in Small School Design* (Oneonta, N.Y.: 215 Home Economics Building, SUTC), 1959.

[10] John G. Cober, "The Development of Types of Public School Business Organization, Personnel in Charge, and Standing Committees Used for Management of Business Affairs as Revealed in School Surveys," (unpublished doctoral dissertation, University of Pittsburgh, 1956).

delegation, communication, coordination, and effective management. In some observations of school central office organizations, the findings appear to indicate that administrators perceived their roles as "doers of tasks," instead of delegators and coordinators, much the same as they had done in small organizations. A man's reach is limited, and as a consequence some tasks remain unaccomplished or poorly accomplished. Big business cannot be effectively operated with small-business concepts and perceptions.

Other attempts to obviate the shortcomings of large central organizations, as in the city of Chicago, have included plans of "decentralization" by the creation of area subdistricts under the supervision of area superintendents. Subdistrict boards and area lay advisory councils to the central administration have been created in some situations. There is evident need for imaginative innovations in making the increasingly larger educational administrative units more effective and efficient.

Demands on the Schools

High on the list of factors affecting the local setting for educational administration are the burgeoning program demands: academic, nonacademic and service. Mere mention of the continuing expansion of knowledge in almost every subject area is a sufficient reminder of its impact on demands and changes in the curriculum. A quick comparison of the high school physics texts of the 1920's and current books used in the subject provides a typical example of change and volume of content. Anderson lists five important factors and conditions affecting trends in educational programs: (1) significant changes that occur in civilization; (2) new discoveries and advances in all sciences; (3) new information on growth and development of children and the learning process; (4) new conceptions and goals and purposes of education; and (5) changes in organization, administration, and financing of education.[11]

Although subsumed in the above factors, the impact of the space age, national security, and national defense have influenced curriculum change. These new and changing academic demands result in a chain reaction of implications too numerous to cover adequately

---

[11] Adopted from Vernon E. Anderson, *Principles and Procedures of Curriculum Improvement* (New York: The Ronald Press Company, 1956), pp. 104–5.

here. More and better instructional equipment is needed; better qualified personnel are required; scheduling and utilization of instructional facilities are affected; the length of the school year and summer school offerings are being reexamined; and in a number of instances the thirteenth and fourteenth years have been added to the public school system. All of these have implications for budget and administration.

Nonacademic and service demands.   Coincidentally, along with the demands for change in the curriculum offerings, have come new demands upon the schools for nonacademic, extracurricular, cocurricular, and service programs. The administration's responsibility for the three B's—beans, busses, and basketball—is more than idle jest. Actually, from the point of view of time consumption, the generation of problems, and public relations difficulties, the nonacademic and service responsibilities of administration have taken on disproportionate dimensions. Regardless of their contributions, these efforts have ceased to be operations done "on the side" and as "extras." These services and programs have come to demand specialized facilities and equipment, trained personnel, exacting building site and space requirements, and supervision and budget considerations.

Transportation of pupils.   Along with the conviction on the part of Americans that all the children of all the people are entitled to free public education came the demand for pupil transportation. Since the early authorization in 1868 by the Massachusetts legislature for transportation of students, the operation has expanded to include all states. Better roads, consolidations, and universal demands for better educational opportunities have been the chief factors in promoting student transportation.

The acquiring, garaging, maintaining, routing, manning, scheduling, insuring, and supervising of school busses have become an added accepted educational administrative responsibility. Needless to say, public education now operates one of the largest transportation businesses in the country.

School lunch program.   Within recent years the school lunch program has become an integral part of most public school programs. It has evolved from a midmorning orange juice or milk program for younger pupils to a full-fledged restaurant operation in many schools.

Among the administrators' concerns attendant to the lunch

program operation are providing space and equipment; food acquisition, storage, preparation, and service; staffing; maintenance; financing; and supervision.

Community recreation program. Although education for wise use of leisure time has long been accepted as a school responsibility, providing recreation programs for youth during nonschool hours and vacation periods is another of the recent community expectations of its school system. The reasoning seemingly has been that since the schools have the playgrounds, gymnasiums, pools, courts, and other facilities (plus some personnel), and since these facilities might well be put to extended use during nonschool periods, the schools may rightfully be called upon to furnish this community service.

School health program. Health education, health inspection of students, immunization programs, dental inspection, summer round-up, baby clinics, first aid, and similar health-related provisions and activities have become more or less standard expectations to be provided for to a major extent by the school system.

Adult education. Upon community insistence, many school systems have initiated programs for adult education. Obviously, in an organization attuned to daytime operations for the education of children and youth, after-school and evening operations for adult education pose separate and somewhat unique administrative problems.

As indicated in the literature, more and more people are realizing that the public schools may well function in the lives of *all the people* of the community.[12] The scope of adult education has come to include a wide variety of experiences commensurate with adult interests. Academic subjects, forums, lectures, shop work, vocational subjects, music, art, and the like are representative of the course offerings in adult education.

Miscellaneous community services. The schools are an integral part of the community and thus share in many projects, services, and observances of a community-wide nature and interest. Problems arise, however, as many groups and organizations in the community turn to the schools for cooperation in their laudable but individual

---

[12] *Community Education: Principles and Practices from World Wide Experience,* Fifty-Eighth Yearbook of the National Society for the Study of Education, Part I (Chicago: The University of Chicago Press, 1959).

group projects. The school music organizations are called upon to perform at meetings; requests are made for participation in a group's essay or poster contest for youth; requests are made to utilize students for door-to-door canvassing for good causes; and so on. In some instances these requests, no doubt unintentionally, exploit students' time which should be preserved for study and school work.

Another pressure upon schools is that of requests for use of school facilities. Although most state school codes have provisions for the priority of use of facilities for school purposes, there are many requests that are lodged with the school administration quite oblivious of constituted priorities. These miscellaneous requests for services, facilities, and school equipment have become an increasing source of concern to educational administrators.

Summary

In a terse manner, this chapter attempts to describe an overview of the situational factors under which educational administration functions. In attempting to cover and generalize on the many and varied local situations in which educational administration operates, no such scintillating review as that of Martin Mayer's letter of welcome to the new New York City superintendent is possible.[13] In the crisp, erudite style of a journalist, Mayer has attempted to describe the situational factors in the setting for school administration in New York City. It does for a single situation what this chapter alludes to for local situations in general.

For a thorough understanding of the setting for administration and organization, situational factors and trends in the locus of operations for educational administration and the formal and legalistic structure discussed in Chapter I should be considered together. The factor of variability in local situations, the trends and inertia developed, traditions, local loyalties, pride, complacency, barriers, demands, economics, value systems, and the like—all generate forces and influences that are uniquely related to all forms of public administration. A recognition of the dynamic nature of the structural and situational settings in which administration operates is important in itself, but it is also significant to the discussions of theory, process, and functions of administration in succeeding chapters.

[13] Martin Mayer, "Welcome to the System," *Harper's* (January, 1963), p. 74.

CHAPTER III

Administrative Functions and Processes

Woodrow Wilson, a political scientist as well as former President of the United States, has been credited with being among the first to define administration in terms of function: the "detailed and systematic execution of public law."[1] In contrast with this early definition, recent students of administration define it as "the coordinating of efforts of people toward the achievement of the goals of the organization." Many forces have influenced the image of administration since Wilson's early definition of the phenomenon in the 1880's. Concepts about the nature of administration have changed, as well as the societal values behind the conceptual developments. These changing values and evolving concepts of administrative functions have had a similar impact and influence for change in the processes of administration.

These developments in educational administration raise some searching questions: What are the emerging mental pictures of administration and administrators? What, if anything, is distinctive about educational administration? Is educational administration becoming a science? How shall we look upon processes involved in administration?

It is the purpose of this chapter to examine briefly (1) the changing conceptions of the work of administration; (2) the changing ideas of the administrators; (3) some unique aspects of educational administration; (4) administrative tasks or functions in education; (5) the processes involved in administration; and (6) some important principles and skills. While a past, present, and future approach to this overview might prove to be highly interesting, this chapter limits itself to a brief backward look, particularly as it relates to the present.

---

[1] Woodrow Wilson, "The Study of Administration," *Political Science Quarterly,* Vol. 2 (June, 1887), p. 97.

Old Perspective of Administration

At the beginning of this century, Professor Goodnow, an early scholar in the field of public administration, proposed that the governmental process consisted of two parts: politics and administration.[2] The distinction between politics and administration has been a subject of considerable debate among political scientists since that time. One distinction appeared to have been established in these early discussions: The function of administration was to carry out and execute faithfully the policies given to it through the political process, while politics was charged with the responsibility of the formulation and enactment of policy. In the context of educational administration, this says that administration should merely execute and carry out policies, and that the policy-making function is to be done by the board of education and the citizens of the community.

Although the arguments continue in some quarters regarding the distinctions between policy making (politics) and administration, the facts bear out the point that administration plays an increasingly active role in development and advocation of public policy. How can public policy be intelligently formulated apart from concern for administrative experience and know-how? Undoubtedly it was this concern and other problems of practicability that led scholars like Willoughby and others to espouse the theory of delegation of administrative supervision to administration.[3] These older perspectives of administration were implemented to a large extent in the early history of educational administration when the selectmen, the committee, or the board of education combined policy making and administration in operating schools, leaving very little administration to be executed by the school administrator.

The history and development of the legal structure for administering education reflect a perspective that holds the board of education accountable for the administration of the schools, even to spelling out detailed duties of members and officers of the boards. Comparatively, the laws of the various states have only recently included specific provisions for delegation of administrative respon-

---

2 Frank J. Goodnow, *Politics and Administration* (New York: The Macmillan Company, 1900).

3 W. F. Willoughby, *Principles of Public Administration* (Baltimore: Johns Hopkins University Press, 1927).

sibilities in education, certification requirements for school administrators, and delineated duties to be performed.

Leadership problems. If the concept of a distinction between politics and administration is accepted as practical and feasible, it must be accepted with one important major assumption: that leadership in the advocacy and adoption of important policies and objectives will be provided by the political element in government, whether in the school system or in municipal, state, or national affairs. Under this concept no provision is made for the administration to advise the political element. The observation might be made at this point that government as related to public education and the local school district is something quite apart from state and federal government. The uniqueness is granted, but the association of school district government with other forms of government and public administration is undeniable; all are public in nature and depend on the citizens for support, election of representatives, and major decisions upon which policy is developed and executed. Similarly, the administration of a school system is different from business administration, even though many of its functions and operations are very much alike. Administration anywhere must be viewed in the context of its operational environment.

All public affairs, including educational affairs, require determined, alert, timely, intelligent, moral and politically responsible leadership.[4] Our system of government expects that this type of leadership will emerge as an amalgam of effort by both political officials and professional administrators. School district government requires strength of leadership on the board of education and in the school administrators. Boards of education are expected to employ the kinds of administrators who will provide strong administrative leadership, who will keep the board continuously informed, and who will provide technical and expert judgments upon which the boards rely for making policy decisions, legislation, and appraisals.

New Perspectives of Administration

The treatment of some of the developmental aspects in adminis-

---

4 John D. Millett, "Perspectives of Public Administration," *Preparing Administrators: New Perspectives* (Columbus, Ohio: University Council for Educational Administration, 1962), p. 21.

tration upon which the newer perceptions of administration are based is deferred to the next chapter, because such a treatment is closely related to the changing nature of the study of administration and the progress made in the study of administration as a social phenomenon. It is also recognized that new perceptions in administration are likewise closely related with the perceptions of the administrator discussed below. Briefly stated, the new perspectives of educational administration are the result of:

1. An effort to characterize administration as a science and an administrator as a professional person;
2. Intensive study of administration as a phenomenon of behaviors, performances, social interactions, human relationships and the like;
3. The application of theory and model constructs to the study of administration;
4. An analysis and differentiation of administration into two dimensions—content and process;
5. A recognition of the new forces that shape new perspectives in administration—new technologies, population phenomena, ideological conflicts and changes in value systems, knowledge explosion, and the like;
6. A mounting interest of scholars and researchers in the scientific study of administration.

The patent result of these modifiers of the perspectives of administration have led to:

1. Studies and definitions of content dimensions;
2. Analysis and definition of process dimensions;
3. The development of a beginning body of scientific knowledge about administration;
4. Experimentation and exploration in methodology for training administrators for administration;
5. The utilization of the contributions from the behavioral sciences in studying administration and administrators;
6. A growing trend toward professionalization on the part of practicing administrators evidenced by standards of preparation, ethics, accreditation actions, membership requirements in professional organizations and the like;
7. A growing body of literature on the subject of administration.

An example of the evidence of change as a result of new perspectives in both business and educational administration is the development in the posture and rigor of undergraduate and graduate programs focused upon administration. Management development programs in industry, now becoming common practice, especially in larger industries, are relatively new innovations. Such concepts as full-time administrators, specialization, in-service education for updating and retraining of administrators, selection for training, and the like are relatively new in education. These and many other evidences of change have resulted in the development of a growing new conception of administration.

The foundations for, and purposes and objectives of, a continuous concern about new perspectives in educational administration are clearly evident in our culture. Competition and survival concerns have placed an entirely new significance on education, technical skills, research, and knowledge. Premiums have been placed on excellence and quality. Automation, cybernation, and advanced technology are making new demands upon education and hence upon the administration of it. The complexity of the environment in which schools must play a significant role continues in a course of ever increasing complications (see Chapter VI).

Perceptions of the Administrator

The perception of administration is irrevocably tied to the image of the administrator. It has been cogently said, "Administration is people"; that is, what we relate to in administration are the persons involved. Therefore, it is fitting that we examine the changes that have taken place in the popular mental picture of the administrator. What is an administrator—tycoon, prince, boss, dictator, manager, expert, coordinator, leader, specialist, generalist, politician, opportunist? Wherein lies his contribution to administration—as an expert on process, a specialist in instruction, an organizer, an expediter, an efficiency expert, a human relations authority, a generalist? Admittedly, the expectations of the administrator are vast and far-flung. His range of responsibilities is wide and varied.

Self-image. Certainly there are several aspects to the image of the administrator. One aspect deals with how others see the administrator; another concept is the self-image. The self-image of the administrator probably includes (1) the image of himself as he really is; (2) what he perceives others think him to be; and (3) the image of himself he would really like to project. It is not a mere rationalization that the administrator sees himself in relation to the dimensions of administration. He sees himself in relation to the tasks (content) of the job, and in relation to how the tasks are accomplished (process). His measures of satisfaction or dissatisfaction, success, or failure are tied intimately to the job to be accomplished and to the ways of achieving the accomplishments. He is, or should be, also perceptive to the various factors, conditions, and environmental complexities that condition his satisfaction and success quotients.

Take, for example, the matter of scheduling one's time as an administrator. A common complaint of the administrator is that he just does not have time to do the things that he feels are the most important, such as working on problems of improving instruction. The frustration arises from the fact that other things like buildings, busses, athletics, and the like take time away from what he deems to be most important. On the other hand, there are school administrators who perceive themselves mainly as builders and business managers and are quite content to proffer this image. In fact communities have been known to seek out the administrator with a good record of successful building experience regardless of his other competencies and qualifications. Other communities seek the services of the instructionally oriented administrator, particularly in suburban areas with high regard for strong instructional programs.

The object here is not to establish the dimensions of either a corporate or self-image of the administrator, but rather to call attention to the fact that perceptions of the administrator are closely related to the perceptions of administration and that these images are changing and evolving. If a speculation were to be made as to what the administrator should be like, it is the opinion of the authors that he would be seen as a "perceptive generalist," a person with broad and inclusive competencies and interests, including some expertness along defined lines.

Unique Aspects of
Educational Administration

Whether or not educational administration has a special uniqueness about it is a much debated question. Arguments have been generated supporting extremes of both positions. The position taken here could be characterized as moderate, recognizing some distinctiveness about administration in education. Contentions supporting this view are outlined below.

It has been noted earlier that educational administration has much in common with public administration, business administration, and administration in various other organizational settings. Although the insights gained in studies of other types of administration have been most helpful and many of the concepts have proven to have universal application for all forms of administration, it is also true that educational administration has a certain uniqueness of function and purpose.

Authorities have generally agreed that there are three levels of systems within organization: technical, managerial, and institutional.[5] Whereas much attention has been paid to the managerial level, the technical and institutional levels have been somewhat neglected. To a major extent, it is in these neglected levels that the uniqueness of educational administration is indicated. Campbell, Corbally, and Ramseyer realized this fact and proposed six elements of a continua related to the special considerations of educational administration.[6]

These elements relate to (1) the services which the organization is designed to provide; (2) the nature of the activity; (3) the characteristics of personnel in the organization; and (4) the societal appraisal of the function and contribution of the organization. The six elements related to the above dimensions are cruciality to society, public visibility and sensitivity, complexity of function, intimacy of necessary relationships, staff professionalization, and difficulty of appraisal. To this list the authors suggest the addition of a seventh element—quality controls.

Cruciality. What services are expected from an educational organization? What services is the organization designed to provide. How do these services relate to the home, the aspirations of parents for their children, the needs for an intelligent electorate, and other societal needs? How crucial are they? This last question is certainly debatable, but, if measured by comparison and degree,

---

[5] Talcott Parsons, "Some Ingredients of a General Theory of Formal Organization" in *Administrative Theory in Education,* ed. Andrew W. Halpin (Chicago: Midwest Administration Center, University of Chicago, 1958), pp. 166–85.

[6] Roald F. Campbell, John E. Corbally, Jr., and John A. Ramseyer, *Introduction to Educational Administration* (Boston: Allyn and Bacon, Inc., 1962), p. 81.

the cruciality of educational organization to society is obviously a consideration at the institutional level.

The suggestion here is that education is crucial to the welfare of society and is unique since it is more crucial than many other types of activities. Some indications appear to be pointing to increased cruciality rather than to a diminishing importance.

Public visibility. The nature of the relation of education to the people is noted from several points of view in this volume. Generally speaking, what goes on in a factory manufacturing bolts in a community is far less visible to the people than what goes on in the schools; fewer people are involved and fewer people have an interest in bolts than in education.

This "goldfish-bowl" existence of schools and their operations has definite implications for educational administration, and it is probably the major difference between public and private organizations.

Complexity of function. The functions performed by some organizations are more technical and more complex than others. While not belittling the complexity of any productive organization, it is clear that teaching and learning subsume greater complexity than, say, operating a sawmill; yet they are less complex than operations and functions of a psychiatric ward. One characteristic of school administration is that it involves more than average technical and complex operations. This complexity leads to many organizational and coordination problems.

Intimacy of necessary relationships. Again, on the technical level, the intimacy of operations and the person-to-person contacts in the operation of a school provide a uniqueness to educational administration. There are teacher-pupil relations, pupil-pupil relations, teacher-teacher relations, teacher-parent relations, pupil-parent relations, administrator-teacher relations, and so on—all involving complex interactions on a day-to-day basis. The personality and character of the student is often involved. Confidences must be respected, and many times fine lines must be drawn between the province of the school and the home, students and teachers, administration and staff, school and community.

Professionalized staff. From the point of view of the managerial level, few organizations equal or surpass the school situation with respect to professionalization of staff personnel. Teachers are required to have certain legal qualifications, preparation, and certification. As a consequence, it seems highly probable that administration must pay more attention to personal dispositions of school staff personnel than would the administration of a factory. Matters such as professional values, articulateness in communication, teacher judgments, and the like serve to contribute to the complexities of administration involving a high degree of professionalization in staff.

Appraisal difficulties. On a continuum at the technical level, appraisal in an educational enterprise is appreciably more difficult and complex than in most other administrative situations. How does one adequately measure change in behavior? How does one measure change involving knowledge, skills, attitudes, and the like? What are the ultimate criteria for measuring the success of an educational enterprise? There are good answers to the questions just raised. Surely, there are ultimate measures and criteria, but they are much more complicated and difficult to execute in contrast with counting the output of a bolt factory.

Appraising the output or success of education requires dealings with many intangibles. It must deal with elusive elements such as what portion of credit can the school claim in the success of a student? How does one determine the impact of the home, church, community, and other forces on the change of personality in the child? These and other factors relating to appraisal certainly contribute to the uniqueness of educational administration.

Quality controls. The administration of most enterprises concerns itself with quality controls—quality of raw materials, quality in processing, quality inspection of the finished product, and the like. Standards are established for raw materials, and items that do not meet specifications are rejected. In contrast, the schools have little to say about what they have to work with. All children are required to go to school and continue in school up to a given age, regardless of whether or not they can profit from the experience. These facts also contribute to the uniqueness of educational administration.

Administrative Functions or Tasks

The development of a rationale for the determination of analysis and the delineation of taxonomies of administrative functions have evolved through several phases. These phases have been related to societal values, to pragmatic experiences of administrators, to the needs structure of business and industrial organizations, and to such practical considerations as efficiency, economy, conservation of human resources, and democracy in administration. The evolution of the rationale has shown a marked relatedness to time and to historical developments. Factors such as the advent of machines, technology, automation, and the increasing complexity of administrative enterprises have also contributed to shaping the images of the functions of administration.

Efficiency and scientific management. The concepts of efficiency and scientific management were among the first to appear in the literature dealing with a scholarly appraisal of the functions of administration. The function of administration was seen as that of getting the job done efficiently. In a climate of rugged competition, the objective was to compete successfully through better efficiency and scientific management. Personnel was considered a mere adjunct to machines in a process of performing routine tasks. Frederick W. Taylor, often called the father of the scientific management movement, noticed that workers were in charge of both planning and performing their jobs.[7] He felt that this led to much waste and inefficiency. His experience led him to formulate his principles of time study, price rate, separation of planning from performance, scientific work methods, managerial control, and functional management. These principles nourished and significantly shaped early concepts of the functions of administration.

Human relations. In the twilight period of extreme individualism and the more or less impersonal aspects of efficiency at all costs, the writings of Mary Parker Follett,[8] Eltom Mayo,[9] and others began to receive acceptance. Thus in the early 1930's human relations and social welfare values began to form the basis for another phase in the determination of the functions of administration. While production and efficiency continued to be a part of the objective of administration, some new and more inclusive dimensions

---

[7] Frederick W. Taylor, *Scientific Management* (New York: Harper & Row, Publishers, 1947).

[8] Mary Parker Follett, *Creative Experience* (New York: Longmans, Green, & Co., Inc., 1924).

[9] Elton Mayo, *The Human Problems of Industrial Civilization* (Boston: Graduate School of Business Administration, Harvard University, 1946).

were added. Functions related to internal operations of the enterprise involving personnel received more attention. While competition remained, movements toward cooperation emerged. Trade associations among competitors were established. The term "democratic administration" was coined during this period. Textbooks on administration appeared with "human relations" in the title—the last one (to the authors' knowledge) in 1956.

"New" science of administration. Recent developments having an impact on the functions of administration may be characterized by a decline of emphasis on "human relations" and the ascendency of an analytic view and scientific values—a new science of administration. Sharp distinctions began to be drawn between philosophy and science, between gathering facts and testing hypotheses as contrasted with prescribing the actions and behaviors involved in the tasks of administration. Textbooks began to discuss the "what" and the "why" of administration in contrast to "principles" and the "how" formulas of the past. Processes in administration received new emphasis. This approach envisioned the possibilities of determining criteria by which the effectiveness of administration could be measured scientifically.

Emphasis on emergence. The preceding brief review of the phases in the emergence of a rationale for determining analysis and delineation of administrative functions serves to highlight the evolutionary nature of the determinants. The end is not in sight for still other approaches to the study of administration are emerging (see Chapter IV). Out of these approaches there will emerge new ways of looking at administrative functions, perhaps new concepts of tasks, and new focuses on purposes and substantive policies. New images of both the administrator and administration are likely results. All this will have a relation to any kind of categorization of the functions and tasks of administration.

Administrative tasks. Administration is a process involving a system of interwoven elements including (1) planning, (2) organization, (3) management, and (4) appraisal and control. A comprehensive understanding of the basic elements of administration is necessary to an appreciation of the tasks in educational administration.

In a global look at administration (whether in education, industry, or government) Halpin says that it refers to a human activity that involves a minimum of four components: (1) the task (tasks), (2) the formal organization, (3) the work group (or work groups), and (4) the leader (or leaders).[10]

The concern here is with the task—that is, the mission of the organization and its reason for being. The over-all task of public schools is to "educate." Administration in this case is to facilitate teaching and learning. Again, this task represents a system of interrelated subtasks. Although theory development and future scientific study may develop a more defensible categorization of the subtasks, the authors accept the seven categories as stated by Campbell, Corbally, Ramseyer, and others.[11] The seven operational task areas are:

1. School-community relationships
2. Curriculum development
3. Pupil personnel
4. Staff personnel
5. Physical facilities
6. Finance and business management
7. Organization and structure

School-community relationships. Education is largely a public venture. To a marked extent the schools in a community are what some leader, group, or citizens want them to be—no better, no worse. Thus the harmony of understanding that exists between the schools and the citizens becomes very important. Administration is faced with the task of initiating and maintaining an effective program of school-community relations.

A realistic approach to the dimensions of this task includes a careful assessment of the characteristics of the community, the general level of approval or disapproval of the school program, a determination of the educational philosophy held by the citizens, the receptivity of the community to change and innovation, an analysis of communication patterns and the effectiveness of communication, weighing of desires and aspirations that citizens have for their schools, building a realistic expectation of what the public

---

[10] Andrew W. Halpin, "A Paradigm for Research on Administrator Behavior," in *Administrative Behavior in Education,* eds. Roald F. Campbell and Russell T. Gregg (New York: Harper & Row, Publishers, 1957), p. 161.

[11] Roald F. Campbell, John E. Corbally, Jr., and John A. Ramseyer, *Introduction to Educational Administration,* 2nd ed. (Boston: Allyn and Bacon, Inc., 1962), Chap. 4.

schools can and should do in the community, organizing an effective program of keeping the citizens informed and providing information, and engendering a commitment on the part of the people for the support of education.

Obviously the task is not merely one of "selling" the schools to the people or of "selling" the program. It involves the establishment of a high level of rapport between the schools and the people, of lifting levels of understanding, of engineering consent and approval, and of maintaining a strong commitment to a quality program of education.

Curriculum development.   This is the task of program development. Program development includes those activities in which school personnel and others engage to plan, carry forward, and evaluate instructional experiences. Curriculum development has to do with what is taught and how it is taught.

Change in instructional content and method occurs when the understanding and skills of teachers and other workers change. The task involves working with people in the development of new insights and skills. These insights and skills are related to the following curriculum categories: determining of objectives, the development of a program of instruction, the use of instructional materials and procedures, and the appraising of instruction.

Determining objectives is an involved process. It involves setting up conditions in the school system and community so that a concept of specific objectives for instruction are developed. How to provide for the gifted, the slow learner, the handicapped, the college bound, and those seeking vocational and technical skills is among the many concerns in establishing objectives for instruction. Opportunities must be provided to learn more about the culture and its demands upon the schools, and to learn more about the growth and development of children. Opportunities for study, research, and program assessment must be encouraged and provided for.

Objectives must be implemented in a program of instruction. Much of this is, of course, the responsibility of teachers in the classrooms, but where system-wide program changes are involved, there is need for cooperative staff action. Many schools have found the use of district-wide curriculum councils helpful in program development.

With all this, the administrator must take the responsibility for arranging for the selection and acquisition of instructional materials. The nature of these materials run the gamut from textbooks to teaching machines, from scientific apparatus to food supplies for home economics. Budget provisions must be made to cover costs of instructional materials. Committees need to be established and the staff needs to be involved in reviewing, appraising, and determining standards for selection. Warehousing, inventory, and distribution of supplies must be planned.

Finally, it becomes the responsibility of the administration to plan and execute a program of appraisal of instruction. The end products and the results of instruction must be measured against the previously established goals and objectives.

Pupil personnel.   Activities included within the operational area of pupil personnel embrace those services to pupils that supplement regular classroom instruction. Included are such important services as pupil inventory and organization, pupil accounting, health services, child study, guidance and counseling, testing, visiting teacher service, social worker services, speech and hearing therapy, control of student behavior, transportation, psychological service, and the like. All these require planning, organization, staffing, budgeting, coordinating, appraisal, and supervision.

Staff personnel.   Staff personnel is one of the major operational areas in educational administration. It deals with providing the human resources to execute the instructional and service programs of the school. Many kinds of personnel are needed in a modern school operation. Among the specific elements in staff personnel administration are (1) the development of personnel policies; (2) recruitment of staff—both certificated and noncertificated; (3) screening, testing, and selecting staff people; (4) orientation of new staff; (5) placement and assignment; (6) supervision and appraisal; (7) personnel records; and (8) various other minutia that accompany employer-employee relationships.

Physical facilities.   School buildings, sites, and equipment needed in and incidental to instruction comprise the major elements in the administrative task of providing for physical facilities. Planning the modern school plant is a major undertaking. It must be functional, flexible, economic, safe, convenient, well-located, program-oriented, well-equipped, well-maintained and so on. Sites have to be carefully chosen and developed. Provisions must be made for parking, play areas, practice fields, outdoor sports, and the many other demands made upon school sites. The task also involves the provisions for major equipment acquisitions, maintenance, and supervision.

Finance and business management. Although closely associated for most purposes and often subsumed under the concept of business affairs in the school district, finance and business management constitute a two-part administrative task. Recent writers in the field describe the task of school finance as those activities which lead to the receipt of moneys and the funding of the educational enterprise. Business management is described as the task that involves those activities dealing with the expenditures and management of school funds, the management of district-owned properties, accounting, and record keeping.

The details of business management in the schools are described in another volume of the Library of Education series. Some of the main elements in this general task area are budget-making, securing revenues, managing expenditures, purchasing, accounting, and often managing noncertificated personnel.

Organization and structure. Organization and structure is the task area that has to do with relations of people and systems contrived to achieve defined goals and purposes. This is a task of administration that has long been recognized but that has received far too little attention and study. Organization and structure have been taken for granted and as something imposed and more or less structured in the practical operations of the enterprise. Only recently has there been much written on the subject, and then only by way of recognition of some of the problems involved. For a comprehensive overview of the subject, the reader is directed to the work of Griffiths, Clark, and others referred to previously in this chapter.

Some of the important elements of the administrative task related to organization and structure include concepts of formal and informal organization, authority patterns, controlling boards, organization for administration, channels of communication, and participation in administration. The formal structure for organization has been described in some detail in Chapter I. Portions of Chapter II deal with the informal organizational structures with which administration must concern itself.

It is conceded here that no form or amount of administrative organization will, by itself, guarantee an effective school system. It is believed, however, that appropriate administrative organization can and will facilitate the achievement of the goals and purposes of the school district. Whether the organization is structured horizontally or vertically, centralized or decentralized, flat or pyramidal depends on a number of factors. Similarly, working with the board of education and lay groups, communication problems, delegations of authority and responsibility, and other problems of organization depend on local factors and the philosophy of administration held by the administrator, the board of education, the staff, and the community.

Some of the signs that point to the need for attention to be paid to administrative organization are, for example, (1) a large portion of administrative time and effort spent on "emergencies"; (2) conflicting orders and decisions; (3) unexplained delays in carrying out plans; (4) frequent complaints such as "I didn't know; no one told me"; and (5) sagging morale. These are symptoms of an ailing organizational structure and a warning that the concepts and principles of administrative organization should be carefully reviewed.

Tenets of Administrative Organization

A discussion of tenets, rules, principles, or guidelines for educational administrative organization should be preceded by appropriate reservations and a proper conceptual framework. The reservations should include (1) that the science of administration, in the degree that it is a science, is very much in its beginning stages; (2) that much of what exists regarding organization has been borrowed from other sources such as the military, business, and industry; (3) that organization is a task area of administration that has received virtually very little scientific study; (4) that the application of theory to the study of organization is in its infancy; (5) that the limited empirical observations of administrative organization to date may not be adequate as a basis for the formulation of well-founded principles and rules; and (6) that any rules or guidelines postulated at this stage should be considered tentative and subject to eventual verification.

Conceptually, the issues and concerns in administrative organization arise from the difficulties of trying to integrate individual and organizational goals. Attempts to achieve the solutions to these difficulties have unearthed a myriad of practical operational questions around issues such as authority patterns, delegation of responsibilities, span of control, tall or flat organizational patterns, centralized and decentralized control, the nearness of controls to operational areas, unit and multiple controls, institutional and individual purposes in organization, and the unique nature of the educational enterprise in these connections.

"Rules" of administrative organization. From the field of public and business administration Bartholomew suggests the following rules of organization:[12]

1. *Administrative work may be most efficiently organized* by function. This is the *doctrine of unity* which holds that all officers engaged in a particular type of work—health, sanitation, welfare—should operate under a single authority. All agencies in certain segments of an organizational structure should have a rather narrowly defined purpose or objective.

2. *Unified direction* should be embodied in the organization. This is the old rule of *unity of command.* A single individual must be ultimately responsible. No subordinate must be subject to the orders of more than one superior. This is known as "the line of responsibility." Somewhere there must be one final answer to any contradictory commands.

3. *Organization may be according to purpose.* Under this arrangement, staff, auxiliary, and line activities will be separated. This is the application of military terminology to administrative operations. While the term "staff" is sometimes used loosely as meaning variously anyone working, the higher officers, and all those not "line," as used here, *staff* means an agency engaged in planning, analysis, and interpretation of facts, determination of problems, consideration of alternative courses of action with a recommendation, and research and advice to a high-ranking official, but an agency that issues no orders, and one that has no operating responsibilities. On the other hand, the auxiliary and line agencies are operating agencies.

4. *Organization on a hierarchical basis.* This is a "vertical" organizational structure that begins at the bottom of the scale with the workers (*production personnel*) and moves upwards through section heads (*first line supervisors*) through division heads (*middle management*) to the agency head (*top management*). These units are differentiated on the basis of levels of authority and responsibility. This arrangement is re-

---

[12] Paul C. Bartholomew, *Public Administration* (Paterson, N.J.: Littlefield, Adams & Co., 1959) pp. 4–8.

ferred to sometimes as the "scalar" or the "hierarchical" organization, another aspect of work specialization.

5. *Organization and social purpose cannot be disassociated.* That is to say that organization is a means and not an end. Organization creates the potential utility of the structure so that it may be used for the benefit of society. Those who deal with organization matters must be aware of psychological, sociological, and anthropological influences on employee sentiments and responses.

6. *There is no single correct form of organization.* Several factors will determine which is the best organization for a particular situation, among them, size of the institution, geography, required division of labor, personnel, and funds available. Moreover, the "best" administrative organization at a given moment may not be the best later as the social organization of the community changes.

7. *"Span of control"* should be definitely considered in organizational structure and practice. *Span of control* is the number and range of direct communication contacts between any executive office and subordinates that can be effectively carried on without delay and confusion. This means simply that there are limits to the number of subordinates who can be effectively supervised by one individual.

"Guidelines" for administrative organizations. In the field of educational administration, Griffiths, Clark, and others have suggested guidelines for administrative organization:

1. The role of the administrative staff in an institution is to create an organization within which the decision-making process can operate effectively. The organization should permit decisions to be made as close to the source of effective action as possible.

2. The administrative staff of an educational institution should be organized to provide individual staff members with as much freedom for initiative as is consistent with efficient operation and prudential controls. Hierarchical levels should be added to the organization with caution, and only when deemed imperative to maintain reasonable control over the institution.

3. The administrative functions and the sources of decision-making in an institution should be organized to provide the machinery for democratic operation and decentralized decision-making.

4. The purpose of organization is to clarify and distribute responsibility and authority among individuals and groups in an orderly fashion consistent with the purposes of the institution. The structure of the institution is determined by the nature of its decision-making process and the organization of the institution should be established to provide for the most effective operation of this process.

5. An institution should be organized with a unitary source of decision-making at its head. Authority and responsibility delegated by the

chief administrator should result in a unitary pattern of decision-making levels among all subordinates in the institution.

6. The administrative organization, by its very structure, should provide for the continuous and cooperative evaluation and redirection of the organization from the standpoint of adequacy (the degree to which goals are reached) and efficiency (the degree to which goals *are reached relative* to the available resources).[13]

The Administrative Process

With the content of educational administration, the jobs to be done (defined earlier in this chapter), it is now necessary to examine the process—the "how" of accomplishment. The key descriptive words in the literature describing the interwoven elements of the process include planning, organizing, managing, coordinating, decision-making, appraising, controlling, commanding, programming, deliberating, and the like. All authorities seem to agree that there is some kind of sequential order for the elements in the process, but the agreement as to what elements are to be included is much less pronounced.

In the field of educational administration the process is referred to as the "decision-making process" or "administrative process"— both connoting a sequential list of elements, steps, or stages. Although either designation may be used to effectively describe the process, for reasons developed below, "administrative process" is used here.

As a background for the consideration of this topic the reader is urged to review the works of Fayol,[14] Gulick,[15] Sears,[16] and Gregg.[17] The first two authors discuss the topic from the point of view of business and industry while the other authors treat it from the point

---

[13] Daniel Griffiths, David L. Clark, D. Richard Wynn, and Laurence Iannaccone, *Organizing Schools for Effective Education* (Danville, Ill.: The Interstate Printers & Publishers, Inc., 1962), pp. 71–72.

[14] See translation by Constance Starrs, *General and Industrial Management* (London: Sir Isaac Pitman and Sons, Ltd., 1949).

[15] Luther Gulick and L. Urwick, eds., *Papers on the Science of Administration* (New York: Institute of Public Administration, 1937).

[16] Jesse B. Sears, *The Nature of the Administrative Process* (New York: McGraw-Hill, Inc., 1950).

[17] Russell T. Gregg, "The Administrative Process," in *Administrative Behavior in Education,* eds. Roald F. Campbell and Russell T. Gregg (New York: Harper & Row, Publishers, 1957), Chap. 8.

of view of educational administration. Some of the common elements recognized by all four authors include planning, organizing, coordinating, and appraising. From a review of the literature one gains two important impressions: (1) administration is essentially a way of working with people, and (2) the procedures in the administrative process are organizationally oriented rather than oriented to the individual.

Although there has been considerable speculation and expostulation as well as theoretical analysis of the administrative process, very little in the way of empirical testing of the phenomenon has taken place. The work of Griffiths and Hemphill, however, deserves special mention. In a comprehensive experiment and study of the performance of 232 elementary school principals, tested under simulated conditions, these men discovered considerable evidence to support a systematization of the administrative process.[18] From what has been learned it seems fair to say that *the administrative process is the way an organization, through working with people, makes decisions and initiates action to achieve its purposes and goals.*

Stages in the Administrative Process

Regardless of how the procedure is viewed or defined—decision making or administrative process—it is a process involving sequential stages. These are orderly stages in a continuum, however interrelated; that is, one cannot start with the resultant and work backward; the direction is toward the resultant. As shown in the DCS project referred to previously, one very significant component of the procedure lies in the deliberative phase of the procedure, the recognition of the problem, gathering and organizing facts and data, weighing alternatives, and eventually coming to a point of decision on a course of action to be taken. To stop at this point, which unfortunately happens in some cases, totally ignores the implementation and assessment phases of the continuum.

The sequential listing of stages in the administrative process,

---

18 John Hemphill, Daniel Griffiths, and Norman Frederickson, *Administrative Performance and Personality* (New York: Bureau of Publications, Teacher's College, Columbia University, 1962). This study is usually referred to as the Development of Criteria of Success in School Administration Project (DCS).

suggested by Burr, Coffield, Jenson, and Neagley, appears to satisfy the complete cycle of the continuum.[19]

1. Deliberating
2. Decision making
3. Programming
4. Stimulating
5. Coordinating
6. Appraising

Each of the stages will be described in the sections to follow. As indicated earlier, the sequential nature of the several stages poses difficulties in making sharp distinctions between the stages. What is described here is a concept of a process, thus making it hard to say with exactness, "Now the administration is programming." There are, however, times in the sequence of stages when one stage will be more obvious than others.

Deliberating. What is the first thing that administration does when faced with a problem? A beginning must be made—one that several steps ahead will result in a hoped for satisfactory solution to the problem, or at least a definite progress toward satisfaction. Deliberation begins at the moment the administration's attention is focused on a problem. Deliberation on what? The dimensions of the problem are determined; facts are gathered on the exact nature of the problem; the gravity of the problem is weighed; and information is collated upon which a decision can be made.

Decision making. A course of action (a decision) is made based upon due deliberation. Alternatives are weighed and a choice is decided upon. All cogitation and speculation culminate in a decision. Thus the major decision is made in the sequence of stages in the administrative process—the decision upon which all minor decisions and other stages of the process depend.

Programming. Once the course of action is decided, it must be planned and programmed for implementation. For example, imagine that after due deliberation the decision has been made that the science program must be improved in the system. What resources are available? What planning is necessary? What provisions in the way of budget, equipment, and instructional materials are

---

[19] James B. Burr, William Coffield, Theodore J. Jenson, and Ross L. Neagley, *Elementary School Administration* (Boston: Allyn and Bacon, Inc., 1963), pp. 398–402.

needed? What staffing may be involved? How are the plans developed and executed? These are some of the elements to be considered in programming.

Stimulating. This stage involves setting the program into operation. This is an important stage in the administrative process, particularly for an administration dedicated to wide involvement of people and democratic action. Interest has to be aroused, commitments sought, and action initiated. Motivation must be encouraged, attitudes built, and activities channeled. In many instances a "selling job" has to be done. This is stimulation.

Coordinating. Successful program implementation must be concerned with harmonious adjustment to the situation and circumstances—coordination. Timing becomes important. Provisions for supplies and resources must be coordinated. Communications must be channeled. Forces, resources, and actions must be aligned to make their most efficient impact. Poor coordination in the administrative process is sure to have an adverse effect on the implementation phase of the sequences in the procedure.

Appraising. The final stage in the continuum is appraising. It completes the cycle in the administrative process and deals with the evaluation of all other stages in the process as well as with the net results. It attempts to measure success or failure and the reasons why. Immediate, short, and long-range impact of the action will be assessed. Things learned through the experience will be noted for recollection in the next round of action, and thus the cycle continues.

Administration Skills

In an overview of images of the work of administration and administrators, administrative functions and processes, and principles of organization, to leave unmentioned the whole area of skills would be a gross oversight. By the same token it is recognized that the subject of skills in administration is deserving of a much more comprehensive treatment than is possible here. While skills are usually identified as accomplishments of individuals, there is some evidence to indicate that administrative teams possess varying degrees of corporate administrative skills.

Why is it that under new management some languishing enterprises appear to flourish and become successful? What new skills have been brought into play? What brings about change that results in success in the same situation in which the previous management seemed not to succeed? There are undoubtedly many factors which contribute to success in management, but administrative skills are definitely among them.

A skill is a developed or acquired ability—a special proficiency. There are many kinds of skills necessary in the successful administration of a school system. Three categories of skills seem to be especially pertinent: conceptual, technical, and human relation skills.

Conceptual skills. Conceptual skill has to do with the proficiency of administration to originate ideas, to sense problems, to think out solutions, and to form opinions. This is a skill that is necessary to do short- and long-range planning, to determine direction, to establish priorities, to make estimates of what is ahead, and to assume a posture of "vision." Conceptual skills make it possible to reduce the "risk factor" to a minimum, or at least to recognize its reality.

All organizations employ this skill on a day-to-day basis in their operations, but some enterprises have deemed the development of this skill important enough to plan special sessions for conceptualization where the administrative teams attend "retreats," "brainstorming sessions," and "think sessions." On a less sophisticated level, planning conferences are held and institutes, clinics, and seminars are organized. In all of these, attempts are made to utilize the best techniques of group process and group dynamics in order to capitalize on the corporate resources of the individuals and the group as a whole. A wise administration will encourage the development and use of the conceptual skills of individuals on the administrative team, but it will also encourage and make use of the corporate skills and resources of the administrative team working as a group.

Technical skills. Techniques, practices, and methods in administration are subject to skill development and proficiency measures. Indeed, each stage in the administrative process depends on skill development for effectiveness. For example, the degree of excellence with which the administration effects appraisal depends upon the skill brought to bear in its execution. The success of recruitment and placement of the worker may in part depend upon the skill in which a job specification was perceived and written. The solution to a very important administrative problem may depend upon the skill with which the problem was perceived, understood, and communicated to the board of education.

Among the many elements requiring technical skill are budgeting, planning for instruction, communication, preparing reports, estimating costs, involving persons in the group process, initiating policy, developing programs such as a public relations program, interviewing, conferring, organizing meetings, preparing agendas, and the host of technical acts related to administration. These are skills that must be developed by the administrator as an individual and the board of education as a group. One reason some boards and administrative teams seemingly handle problems more effectively than others is that they have developed better technical skills of operation.

Human relations skills.   Human relations skills have to do with getting along successfully with people and eliciting their effective and cooperative efforts and production. It involves proficiency in recognizing and working with persons as individuals; it involves engineering consent. Good human relations skills encourage the individual not only to produce, but also to grow as an individual and a producer in the process. These skills are related to morale building, satisfactions of the producer and the consumer, mutual confidence and respect, and good interpersonal relations.

Although "the one big happy family" concept may seem trite as a description for the objective of good human relations skills and practices, it is toward this goal that efforts to improve proficiencies in human relations skills are directed.

Summary

A review of the administrative functions and processes in education, once thought of as a combination of art and science, indicates a trend toward the establishment of administration as a science. The images of both administration and the administrator have evolved from comparatively simple concepts to increasingly sophisticated entities. It has been suggested that educational administration has certain elements of distinctiveness in comparison with business and industrial administration.

The distinctiveness of educational administration is demonstrated in its unique functions and tasks. Although the administrative process, with its several sequential stages, has universal application in administration, it is particularly adapted to the administration of the educational enterprise involving administrators, boards, staffs, and citizens. In the last analysis, what is considered to be good administration is governed by a defined set of principles and is dependent in a large measure upon the application of sound administrative skills.

CHAPTER IV

The Changing Nature of the Study of Educational Administration

Since the 1950's, the study of educational administration has been undergoing a period of ferment. The change can be observed in the content of the textbooks used for preparing school administrators, the substance of professional meetings, the research being conducted, and the scholarly writings of students of the field. Halpin notes that what he calls a "quiet revolution" has been taking place. He suggests that prior to World War II, "What was taught on administration *qua* administration consisted of maxims, exhortations, and several innocuous variations on the theme of the Golden Rule. The material was speculative rather than theoretical in the true sense of the term. . . . The professors [of educational administration] sought help from psychologists and sociologists, and discovered that without the support of an explicit theoretical framework their discipline could easily degenerate into a jumble of inert facts."[1]

In effect, a new phase in educational administration has been reached which highlights the role of theory in studying and practicing administration. A brief but provocative and influential monograph by Coladarci and Getzels, published in 1955, can be identified as the herald of this new era. The central theme of this document, which pointed the way for much of the work which has followed, was that, "(1) theory and practice constitute an integrity—that is, they are not different things; most commonly they represent differences in the point at which interest and attention are momentarily directed; (2) theorizing is always present in human behavior, if only implicitly, and an explicit concern for theory is necessary to and has patent values for successful practice—indeed, without a theoretical dimension, practice can be only accidentally success-

---

[1] Andrew W. Halpin, "Ways of Knowing," in *Administrative Theory as a Guide to Action*, eds. Roald F. Campbell and James M. Lipham (Chicago: Midwest Administration Center, University of Chicago, 1960), p. 4.

ful."[2] Anyone who hopes to be familiar with the current and upcoming developments in educational administration will be well advised to follow carefully the emerging emphasis on administrative theory in education.

Administration—Art or Science?

Halpin, Coladarci, and Getzels were saying that administration must be viewed as a field of applied science to which the methods of scientific inquiry can be applied if there is to be any hope of continuing progress and improvement in the field. This is a revolutionary concept, since administration has been viewed typically as a subtle art form with success in its practice depending primarily upon qualities of natural leadership which are improved as the administrator accumulates experience.

The administrator as an artist. There is little point, and no intention on the part of the authors, to construct a straw man for subsequent abuse in this chapter. The contention that there has been in recent years a significant number of people who denied the existence of some aspects of a science of administration would indeed be irrelevant. The important question is the relative emphasis placed on the concepts "art" and "science" as they apply to administration. Two examples may be sufficient to illustrate the predominant role which has been assumed by the artist concept in much of the research and study of administration in the past.

One of the major texts in public administration (published about ten years ago and well-respected for its citations of research studies) reveals (1) no systematic treatment of theory as a component of what is known about administration; (2) the division of the field of administration into two parts, "The Art of Administration" and "The Science of Organization"; and (3) only three indexed references to the word theory, one of which was disparaging and the other two of which took up less than a paragraph in a 650 page book.[3]

Within the area of educational administration, the emphasis on artistry can be illustrated by the proliferation of administrator's

---

[2] Arthur P. Coladarci and Jacob W. Getzels, *The Use of Theory in Educational Administration* (Stanford, Calif.: Stanford University Press, 1955), p. 4.

[3] Albert Lepawsky, *Administration* (New York: Alfred A. Knopf, Inc., 1949).

traits studies. Certainly, at least a part of the motivation for these efforts grew from either the concept of the administrator as a "born leader" or the notion that identifiable traits allowed the administrator to practice and perfect his art in a successful fashion.

The impact of this point of view has had many ramifications in educational administration. It has tended to create a chasm between the administrative practitioner and researchers in administration; it has fostered the theory-versus-practice dichotomy; it has stimulated "prescription type" research and depressed theoretical research efforts; and it has placed discernible and finite limits on the improvement of administration, those limits being the extent to which an administrator can learn to do better the things he already knows how to do.

Griffiths has stated this position forcefully in drawing an analogy with the practice of medicine. "The administrator is an applier of science in much the same sense as is an engineer or doctor. There will always be some art in administration, as there is in engineering or medicine; but the amount of art will decrease as the amount of available scientific information replaces administrative folklore. It is true that the present-day doctor is far superior to the 19th century physician, but only because the amount of scientific knowledge available to him is so much greater, not because he is a superior artist."[4]

The origins of the artist movement in educational administration are easy to trace. In the early period of educational development in this country there was little or no recognition given to administration in any form. As Guba points out, "The emphasis . . . was clearly upon the adjective 'educational' rather than upon the noun 'administration,' as is exemplified by the executive titles that came to be used: the title 'principal' is of course shortening of the term 'principal teacher.' . . ."[5] Even as greater recognition was given to the functions of administering by establishing full time administrative positions, it is hardly surprising that the concept of the master

---

[4] Daniel E. Griffiths, *Administrative Theory* (New York: Appleton-Century-Crofts, Inc., 1959), p. 24.

[5] Egon G. Guba, "Research in Internal Administration—What Do We Know?" in *Administrative Theory As a Guide to Action,* eds. Roald F. Campbell and James M. Lipham (Chicago: Midwest Administration Center, University of Chicago, 1960), p. 115.

or principal teacher impeded the development of an emphasis on administration *qua* administration.

The first emergence of scientific administration. The first significant manifestation of concern for educational administration as a science emerged in response to the scientific management concept in business and industry—the rise of the so-called efficiency expert. In its time, this movement could have been identified and discussed in many of the same terms being employed today in assessing the impact of theory development in educational administration. As a matter of fact, this movement had a theoretical framework which was based on a model of the school as a machine with a definable input (students), a system of production (the educational process), and a measurable output (student attainment). As in the case of all theories (as we shall see later in the chapter when discussing some contemporary theoretical formulations), the scientific management theory was incomplete—that is, it failed to account for all the relevant phenomena in educational administration. The educational efficiency experts, however, often employed their theory as if it did explain the whole of administration. This had several unfortunate consequences. First, the theory could never be adequately developed, tested, or evaluated because the bounds of its theoretical scope were not defined. Second, the application of a perfectly acceptable but incomplete theory to the practice of administration led to abuses and disenchantment with not only the theory, but also science in general as it was applied to administration. Third, the consequence of the disillusionment was a revival of the concept of administration as an art form.

The revival of artistry. A major blow was struck at the development of a science of administration by a group of scientists who were, in fact, pursuing their science in an objective fashion. At the Hawthorne Plant of the Western Electric Company in Cicero, Illinois, the now famous studies of illumination and other technical working arrangements were being conducted in the late 1920's and early 1930's. Only one conclusion could be drawn from these investigations: In the field of administration, there were operative human attitudinal factors of such power that the simple machine model and the research derived from it were inadequate to account for the production results attained.

These investigations might well have led to a rapid advance in administrative science either by adding a significant but ignored dimension to an extant theory or by supplanting the machine model entirely with a more sophisticated theoretical formulation. However, this was not the immediate consequence. Despite the fact that in retrospect the scientific management group can be credited with the use of a model and the construction of a theoretical framework, they had, in fact, relatively little explicitly stated theory to support the movement, and they had not faced the question of the use of theory in the development of a science of administration. Consequently, the immediate impact of the Hawthorne studies, and the introduction of what might be called the human relations phase in administration, seemed to have the effect in education of mesmerizing the profession around an ill-defined concept termed "democratic administration." A theory was rejected, but another theory did not rise to take its place.

This era, which continued into the years following World War II, found little attention being paid to research and literally none to the development of administrative theory. It was apparent to the practicing administrator that what was being talked about in college classrooms (and often labeled theory) did not correspond to what he was experiencing on the job. Stated in extreme terms, the substance of administration courses consisted almost entirely of exhortations to involve everybody in everything—be a good, sensitive, human being and it will all work out in the end. The fact that it did not all work out in the end was thought to be proof that the administrator was not as skilled in his human relations as he might have been; his art form left something to be desired.

The emergence of administrative theory. This was the situation in the early 1950's in school administration, but there were many persons who were not satisfied with the *status quo*. These dissatisfactions led to the formation of the National Conference of Professors of Educational Administration, the Cooperative Program in Educational Administration, the University Council for Educational Administration, and to the ferment in the field noted earlier in this chapter. Following the publication of the Coladarci and Getzels monograph which, in addition to advocating the integrity of theory and practice, outlined a theory of administration, there appeared a number of theoretical structures for use in the study of administration. Just as important, perhaps, is the fact that a body of literature grew up which considered the question of the use of theory *per se* in the study and practice of administration and which attempted to establish some commonly accepted definitions for the basic terminology of theory construction. The era of developing an administrative science on a theoretical base had begun.

Theory—The Key to a Science of Administration

Griffiths notes, "It is the aim of science to accomplish three things concerning its subject matter: description, explanation, and prediction."[6] These three words illustrate admirably the reason why theory is the key to a science of administration. The process of describing means simply that some phenomena are observed and that these observations are recorded systematically so that they describe the action and/or interaction which was being observed. But what does one observe, and how are the observations recorded systematically? Obviously the observer must have a vantage point for his observation. This vantage point may be a rather formal theoretical framework or a more general logical structure. In either case, however, the framework or structure must exist unless one is willing to gather data aimlessly until something emerges. Explanation is the business of theory. The purpose of theory is to explain the interrelationships among phenomena. And why? To achieve the final aim of science—that is, prediction—to predict the anticipated and unanticipated consequences of a particular action or set of actions. Theory is the *sine qua non* of science. It is the element which transforms common sense and best guesses to predictive probabilities.

An interesting illustration of the force of theory, or rather the lack of force, in a discipline when theory is missing was provided by a recent research study of classroom-teacher performance skills. A group of elementary school teachers were presented with the actual results of an arithmetic test. The teachers were asked to identify the errors made by the students, classify them as random or systematic errors, and propose a teaching strategy appropriate to overcome those systematic errors which they could identify. Among

---

[6] Griffiths, *Administrative Theory*, p. 22.

the teachers who could identify the systematic errors (and this did not include all the teachers), the predominant response in regard to reteaching the material was to follow the same technique used the first time—but to go over the material more slowly.[7] These teachers did not have available for their use a theoretical structure which would relate varying actions on the part of the teacher to anticipated learning consequences. Presented with symptoms they could not, like a practicing doctor can so often do, elect alternate strategies to attack the symptoms if an initial strategy is unsuccessful. They were, in effect, acting toward the situation in the same way that a layman might act if presented with the same problem. They had no device available to describe in precise language the situation with which they were confronted and to prescribe what was to be done about it. The success of their prescription would be accidental or intuitive rather than scientific; they had no theoretical framework on which to proceed.

The theorists and the practical men. To create the impression that the practitioner of educational administration and all the professors and students of administration are currently embracing enthusiastically the emergence of administrative theory would be to mislead the reader. The bias of the authors is quite clearly exhibited in the last two paragraphs, but it is impossible to deny that theory has long been held in disrepute by practitioners in education. It has been common practice for educators to "devastate" a college course which they have taken by referring to the fact that it was "theoretical" rather than "practical." A large city superintendent reflected the attitude of many educators when he was quoted recently on his attitude toward progressive education. After citing a number of the ideals of progressive education which he stated were admirable, he went on to say, "That's all good theory, but there comes a time when you have to say, 'Look, Sonny, this you have to learn.' "

This quotation illustrates well the place which theory has held in education in general and in school administration in particular. Theory and practice have been treated as a dichotomy, and the initiation rites of the neophyte to the field have included elaborate warnings in regard to the confusion of these two components of his

---

[7] Richard L. Turner and Nicholas A. Fattu, *Problem Solving Proficiency Among Elementary School Teachers: I The Development of Criteria* (Bloomington, Indiana: Institute of Educational Research, 1960).

knowledge. Griffiths illustrates this point by asking a question, "Suppose that someone should say to you, 'This is a very sound theoretical statement.' How would you react? Would you feel reassured? . . . Would you feel that because the statement was theoretically sound it must necessarily be impractical and, therefore, useless? The latter point of view, that theory is useless, appears to be the one most prevalent in the field of educational administration at the present time."[8]

There is still an unbridged gap between the "theorists" and the "practical men" which is impeding the development, testing, and use of administrative theory. Why should this be so? There seem to be a number of reasons ranging from tradition to communication problems.

Impediments to the acceptance of administrative theory. Webster's Dictionary provides a substantial clue to the confusion surrounding theory by noting that in ordinary usage theory can mean "opposed to practice, sometimes to fact." This is certainly what the practitioner means in most instances when he refers to a college course being theoretical rather than practical. This common usage is, of course, not at all what is meant by the word as it is being used by the administrative theorists who are, quite to the contrary, attempting to explain practice through theory.

A second confusion is what Halpin refers to as the confoundment of the "is's" and the "ought's" of behavior.[9] The careless use of the term theory in education has often meant that a description of what someone believes "ought to be" is labeled theory. By any reasonable scientific definition, theory could only deal with the "is's." Since the "is's" and the "ought's" are almost always in conflict, the practitioner has assumed that theory does not explain, but rather contradicts, practice.

The incompleteness of theory also provokes misunderstanding on the part of practitioners. No present theory in administration describes the total reality of the administrative situation and none is likely to in the near future. The practitioner examining a theoretical formulation, however, may expect the theory to be complete and,

---

[8] Griffiths, *Administrative Theory*, p. 7.
[9] Andrew W. Halpin, "The Development of Theory in Educational Administration," in *Administrative Theory in Education*, ed. Andrew W. Halpin (Chicago: Midwest Administration Center, Universty of Chcago, 1958), p. 6.

not finding it so, may assume that the theorizer is unfamiliar with the reality of administration.

Summarizing and supplementing Coladarci and Getzels' explanation of the antitheoretical bias among educational practitioners, Griffiths cites six reasons for the existence of the bias:[10]

1. Factualism: the feeling that all that is required to improve administration is the accumulation of enough facts about administration.

2. Authority: the tendency in educational administration to appeal to the authority of persons to support ideas in contra-distinction to empirical investigation of ideas.

3. Fear of Theory: the fear that theory is too difficult to understand, too hard to use, impractical.

4. Inadequate Professional Language: the lack of well-defined concepts to allow the development of an understood, nonconfusing language of administration.

5. Emotional Identification with Personal Views: the inability to state a theory in nonpersonalized terms. Ideas become so attached to individuals that to examine the idea is to attack the person.

6. Lack of Understanding of Theory: the reflection of the cultural bias which derides research and theory and extols the practical man.

Recent publications in the field of administrative theory, alterations in programs of preparation for school administrators, and a more vigorous effort to bring theorists and practitioners together to discuss theory are having a significant, although hardly revolutionary, impact on the antitheoretical bias. One practical school man, a superintendent of schools who participated in a joint conference of school administrators, social scientists, and professors of school administration, states:

> Disciplined by the preparation of this paper, I have found myself suddenly confronted with an array of information which I have been running too fast to read—or even to know about, except superficially. This selective overview of the literature, therefore, may move you, as it has moved me, to reconsider our posture as "practical" school men and listen with some respect to the theorists.[11]

This is the harbinger of the future for the school administrator who will be affected profoundly by the impact of theory on the practice of school administration.

---

[10] Griffiths, *Administrative Theory*, pp. 8–13.

[11] Sidney P. Marland, "Superintendent's Concerns about Research Applications in Educational Administration," in *Administrative Theory as a Guide to Action*, eds. Roald F. Campbell and James M. Lipham (Chicago: Midwest Administration Center, University of Chicago, 1960), pp. 27–28.

What is theory? Before turning to some of the practical implications of theory which will affect the school administrator of the future, it might be wise to pause briefly for an explicit definition of some of the common language of theory which has been dealt with implicitly up to this point. First, consider the word *theory* itself. Griffiths has proffered a definition which has gained wide acceptance: "A theory is essentially a set of assumptions from which a set of empirical laws (principles) may be derived."[12] In amplification of this definition, Griffiths discusses in some detail what theory is not, and since this discussion covers some of the most common misconceptions of what theory is, it may be worth summarizing briefly.[13]

First, he notes that theory is not a personal affair; that is, although one must assume that an administrator has some basis on which he makes decisions, it is not at all reasonable to assume that this constitutes a theory of administration. Perhaps it is better typified as the individual's administrative style.

Second, theory is not a dream or flight of fancy. It is not, as was stated earlier, whimsy opposed to practice and/or fact. A "bull session," for example, is often labeled theoretical, but it is more appropriately labeled simply a "bull session."

Third, theory is not a philosophy. This was discussed earlier in reference to Halpin's "is" and "ought" confoundment. Philosophy deals with values; theory deals with propositions of fact. Griffiths illustrates from Simon in making this distinction clear:

> In the realm of economics, the proposition, "Alternative A is good" may be translated into two propositions, one of them ethical, the other factual:
>
> "Alternative A will lead to maximum profit."
> "To maximize profit is good."
>
> The first of these sentences has no ethical content and is a sentence of the practical science of business. The second sentence is an ethical imperative, and has no place in any science.
>
> Science cannot tell whether we ought to maximize profit. It can merely tell us under what conditions this maximization will occur, and what the consequences of maximization will be.[14]

---

[12] Griffiths, *Administrative Theory*, p. 28.
[13] *Ibid.*, pp. 13–19.
[14] Herbert A. Simon, *Administrative Behavior* (New York: The Macmillan Company, 1950), pp. 249–50.

Finally, a theory is not a taxonomy. A taxonomy is a classification system. It does not attempt to explain the action or interaction of phenomena, but rather to organize systematically the components of a science.

Before leaving this defining section, reference should be made to a common term associated with theory construction—*models*. This term has both a general and a specific definition which are significant for theory construction. In its general sense, *model* can be used to connote a schema, paradigm, or classification which attempts to describe phenomena in a systematic manner through the use of symbols or classificatory categories, and which when applied to the study of the phenomena are designed to be productive of relevant, testable hypotheses.

Model may also be defined in terms of the isomorphic relation of phenomenon or concept to another. In this context, a model of a well-defined phenomenon or concept is employed to develop hypotheses, laws, or theories regarding a less well-understood area. Earlier in this chapter reference was made to the use of the machine model by the scientific management group in developing theories applicable to the practice of administration. A great deal was known about machine operation; little was known about the practice of administration. The use of the model suggested theoretical postulations in the lesser known area. Both for the further discussion of theoretical formulations and for the discussion of administrative research, it will be useful to understand models and to know how they can be used to generate both theory and research.

Implications of theory for the practice and study of administration. Coladarci and Getzels organize their presentation of the practical implications of theory into two major blocks: implications for the practitioner and for the researcher. In regard to the former they point out that "the educator who behaves on a hit-or-miss basis, one whose professional arsenal consists merely of pat techniques for specific situations is operating in intellectual low gear and is denied the self-initiated, self-critical inquiry and innovation that are possible with the wider frame-of-reference available to the theory-conscious or thoughtful practitioner. Intelligent action, in any sense of that adjective, cannot be maximized without some guiding principles tentatively held."[15] In relation to the researcher they point out that theory systematizes fact gathering and provides a focus for selecting what facts to gather. Theory provides the guiding principles which point the way "to *what* to observe, *what* to measure, *how* to interpret."[16]

Griffiths suggests four implications of theory for the practice and study of administration: (1) as a guide to action, (2) as a guide to the collection of facts, (3) as a guide to new knowledge, and (4) as a guide to explain the nature of administration.[17] In expanding on Coladarci and Getzels' points, Griffiths notes that theory can be employed by the researcher to suggest further testable hypotheses as well as to direct the gathering of facts. In relation to the nature of administration he is emphasizing the explanatory function of theory, suggesting that the employment of theory in the study of administration may lead to a better understanding of what administration is.

Thompson emphasizes the implications of theory for the training of future administrators. He points out, "An adequate theory would equip the future administrator to alter the values of those variables subject to his control as other variables beyond his control change in value. Rather than describing currently accepted practices, an adequate theory would explain why such practices work and why they might not work, if and when the surrounding context changes."[18] He notes, for example, that the paternalistic supervision which was considered desirable administrative behavior forty years ago is considered undesirable today. If that pattern of administrative behavior was learned as an acceptable practice, its unacceptability becomes a difficult problem in adjustment for the administrator. If, however, supervision as an administrative function had been considered within a theoretical structure which encompassed the employees to be supervised as a variable, the unacceptability of the more traditional concept might be easy to adjust to as the administrator considers the change in the variable (in this case, the teacher)

---

15 Coladarci and Getzels, *The Use of Theory in Educational Administration*, p. 7.

16 *Ibid.*, p. 7.

17 Griffiths, *Administrative Theory*, pp. 25–27.

18 James D. Thompson, "Modern Approaches to Theory in Administration," in *Administrative Theory in Education*, ed. Andrew W. Halpin (Chicago: Midwest Administration Center, University of Chcago, 1958), p. 22.

in terms of additional training, the professional organization of teaching, and the increasing cultural emphasis on the human dignity of the individual.

One final illustration of the practical implications of theory may be useful and interesting since it assumed one of the most practical of the school administrator's problems—school building planning —and indicated the impact which educational theory has had on that area. The author of the case, Jacob Getzels, labels it "the case of the changing school chair."[19]

The case begins at the turn of the century when education was profoundly influenced by connectionist psychology—the concept of the learner as an empty organism responding directly to stimuli which were controlled by the experimenter—in this case, the teacher. What could have been more natural than the establishment of rigid learning positions for the students—chairs fastened to the floor—and a teacher-controlled learning situation represented by the teacher's desk set at the head of the classroom, usually on a dais?

How then did educational administrators, who made the decision to have a fixed, teacher-centered classroom, move to today's flexible classroom situation? Getzels suggests that in the ensuing years it became obvious through research and theory in learning that (1) the organism was neither empty nor passive, (2) the learner affected his environment and the stimuli presented to him and, in fact, selected among the available stimuli, and (3) personality variables affected learning. The teacher-centered classroom concept gave way to a child-centered concept, and administrative decisions followed suit by removing the dais and freeing the learner's position through the use of movable chairs.

Finally, Getzels suggests that additional research and theory in group process and group dynamics have had more recent impact on school building planning and furniture placement through a developing concept of a group-centered classroom. This has resulted in the addition of conference tables in the classroom, small group seminar spaces in school buildings, and the inclusion of desks that

---

[19] Jacob W. Getzels, "Theory and Practice in Educational Administration: An Old Question Revisited," in *Administrative Theory as a Guide to Action*, eds. Roald F. Campbell and James M. Lipham (Chicago: Midwest Administration Center, University of Chicago, 1960), pp. 43–58.

can be regrouped within the classroom in conference and group-type arrangements.

Theory has had marked impact on educational developments. Systematic attention to administrative theory indicates that the next few years will find major changes occurring in the practice of, study of, and preparation for school administration.

Theoretical Formulations—A Status Report

The *Review of Educational Research* is often an accurate measure of the stage of development of a topical or methodological area in educational research. Once every three years an issue is devoted to educational administration. A glance at the treatment of theory in the 1955, 1958, and 1961 issues of the *Review* is revealing. In 1955 there was no explicit reference to theory in the chapter headings, but Chase and Guba introduced some of the recent theoretical developments under the heading "Administrative Roles and Behavior."[20] In emphasizing the burgeoning interest in human relations research they noted: "As a part of this development, the application of theory to the investigation of administrative phenomena has achieved increasingly higher valuation."[21] In support of this statement they cited the Coladarci-Getzels monograph and discussed two theoretical formulations and one model. The overwhelming emphasis in their discussion of theory revolved around role theory which had attained considerable popularity and was being used extensively.

By 1958, and continuing through 1961, a discernible change had taken place in the treatment given to theory in the *Review*. Theory was explicitly noted in the chapter titles: for example, the 1958 *Review* chapter by Griffiths and Iannaccone was called "Administrative Theory, Relationships and Preparation," and the diversity of theoretical formulations being discussed had broadened considerably. Griffiths and Iannaccone noted in 1958: "Where three years ago there was reported but one study which pleaded for less naked empiricism and a turn toward theory in research, there [are] now

---

[20] Francis S. Chase and Egon G. Guba, "Administrative Roles and Behavior," *Review of Educational Research*, XXV, No. 4 (1955), pp. 281–98.
[21] *Ibid*, pp. 281–82.

several."[22] They added, "Educational literature also saw the introduction of methodological studies in theory during this period."[23]

Griffiths and Iannaccone (and Campbell and Faber who dealt with the topic of theory in the 1961 *Review*), in addition to continuing the reporting on role theory, also included reports on decision-making theory, formal organization theory, application of several sociological bases for theory-organizational goals, interpersonal relationships, social class, and power structure-social systems theory, and organizational behavior theory. Campbell and Faber concluded: "The recent emphasis on theory in administration continues. Often the theoretical constructs are developed by scholars in the social science disciplines. These formulations, however, are being considered, and at times adapted, by students in educational administration. Even practitioners are becoming aware of theory development and are indicating some readiness to find out what theoretical formulations hold for them."[24]

We are now at a point where a number of provocative theoretical formulations have been posed and are being developed. Much, of course, still needs to be done. The field requires an improved taxonomic base so that theorists can communicate with one another and with practitioners in more precise terms. The existing theories have not been tested empirically in any adequate sense. It is difficult, therefore, to discern which models or theories might have "staying power" to influence future research, theory, and practice. Certainly the field is in need of more extensive and comprehensive theoretical formulations but, perhaps, these await the improvement of our classification and definition systems in administration and the testing of current theories.

To understand the developments to date, the reader needs to examine some of the current models and theories in detail. Obviously they cannot be presented in detailed fashion here, but the authors have selected two samples to illustrate the nature and the form of these theoretical formulations. These are not presented as repre-

---

[22] Daniel E. Griffiths and Laurence Iannaccone, "Administrative Theory, Relationships, and Preparation," *Review of Educational Research,* XXVIII, No. 4 (1958), p. 335.

[23] *Ibid.,* p. 335.

[24] Roald F. Campbell and Charles F. Faber, "Administrative Behavior: Theory and Research," *Review of Educational Research,* XXXI, No. 4 (1961), pp. 363–64.

sentative theories; there is no such theory. Theories by their nature are unique. There are, however, certain common characteristics in the format of theoretical formulations and, more important, there is no better method to introduce the reader to the significance of theory than to ask him to examine a model or theory in terms of what it does for him. Does it help him to organize his thinking about administration? Does it provoke him to raise researchable questions or hypotheses? Does it suggest interrelationships which had not occurred to him previously? In short, does it have heuristic value for him?

In considering these illustrations, the reader would do well to keep in mind an admonition by Halpin which is especially appropriate in the infancy of administrative theory development, but is always appropriate in considering theories. He suggests that we must ". . . guard against a search for *the* theory of educational administration and . . . recognize the possibility of alternative explanations. . . . Thus, as various theories of administration are presented to us, we need not ask, which is right. Each may help us make better predictions of events, and for this reason may appear 'good' or 'right.' "[25]

Illustrations of theoretical formulations. Two quite different theoretical formulations have been selected for presentation. The first, which has been called the tri-dimensional concept of administration, was an early effort in the administrative theory field which grew out of the work of the Cooperative Program in Educational Administration. You will note that it conforms to the more general definition of a model as a schema, paradigm, or classification which attempts to describe phenomena in a systematic manner through the use of symbols or classificatory categories. It is not, in the way in which the machine model was, an isomorphic model.[26]

The second illustration is an attempt to state a theory of administration as decision making. This is a widely disseminated and discussed theoretical formulation which has been constructed by its author not only as a substantive contribution to knowledge about

---

[25] Halpin, "The Development of Theory in Educational Administration," in *Administrative Theory in Education,* pp. 16–17.

[26] The discussion of the tri-dimensional concept in this section is based on *A Developing Concept of the Superintendency in Education* (New York: Cooperative Program in Educational Administration Administrative Center, Teachers College, Columbia University, 1955).

administration, but also to demonstrate the nature and format which
will be required to meet minimal scientific standards in theory development in administration.[27]

The tri-dimensional concept.   The staff of the Cooperative Program in Educational Administration, Middle Atlantic Region, was
not charged with theory development in administration as a central
task in their work. Their purposes were much more action-oriented,
revolving around improved programs of preparation, certification,
and in-service education for administrators. The notion of developing a model to account for the variables affecting the job of the chief
school administrator became a necessity, however, since there was
no existing logical or empirical base on which to project the practical improvements with which they were charged.

How would one go about revising or improving the preparation
program for school administrators? What would one need to know?
Certainly it would be necessary to understand the performance skills
required of the educational administrator—that is, the content of
the job. That is not all that one would need to know, however. The
practice of administration assumes that a man is dealing with the
content of the job in some way. To understand the nature of this
administrative task, the nature of the man on the job would have
to be considered. The man, of course, does not perform the job in
a vacuum; there is a setting within which the man operates on the
job.

These three elements became the model of school administration
on which the Cooperative Program in Educational Administration
began its program of improvement in educational administration:
the job, the man, and the social setting. In considering the content
of the job of educational administration the model set forth four
major substantive aspects:

1. Improving educational opportunity.
2. Obtaining and developing personnel.
3. Providing and maintaining funds and facilities.
4. Maintaining effective interrelationships with the community.

These aspects of the content of the job should meet the criteria of
necessity and sufficiency; that is, they should represent relevant and

---

[27] The discussion of administration as decision making in this section is based
on Daniel E. Griffiths, *Adminstrative Theory,* pp. 71–91.

critical aspects of the content of the job on the one hand, and they should be all inclusive on the other. There should be no dimensions of the job which fall outside the categories.

If the formulation had stopped at this point, it could hardly be termed a model. It would represent an effort at classification, but no interaction would be described. The model, however, proceeds beyond this level to attempt to ascribe process aspects to the job of the administrator and to place these processes in a sequence or time in which the interaction between content and process occurs. The process dimension is divided into the following four segments:

1. Sensing the problem and surveying its aspects.
2. Relating the problem to people.
3. Making decisions.
4. Implementing and reviewing the decisions.

This process which is applied to the content aspects of the job takes place in a time sequence which is classified under the headings past, present, transition, and future.

Thus, presenting the administrator's job schematically, one would derive a 4 x 4 x 4 model as follows:

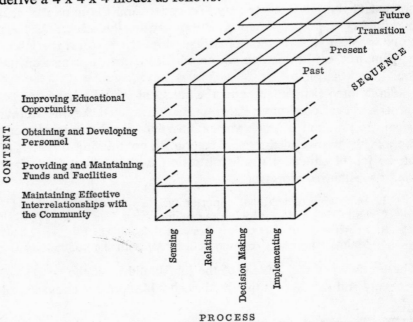

Figure 3. The Tri-Dimensional Concept–Job of the Educational Administrator.

There are two ways in which this model can be assessed. It can be tested empirically to determine the extent to which it does meet the criteria of necessity and sufficiency, and it can be tested heuristically. What it shows can be derived specifically by looking at a single block. Taking the first block in the upper left-hand corner, the model contends that a basic substantive problem for the school administrator lies in the area of the improvement of educational opportunity. The administrator is constantly forced to sense problems in this area and survey their aspects. His activities in this regard are occurring in a dynamic time sequence which has its roots in the past and its implications in the future. Does this help you in any way to sort out your thoughts about administration? If it does this aspect of the model has passed its first heuristic test.

The other two aspects of the tri-dimensional concept are organized in a similar fashion. The next over-all subdivision is "the man." The first dimension of this aspect is the capacity of the man—spiritual, emotional, intellectual, and physical. The second dimension is the behavior of the man—sensing the problem and data collection, making inferences, relating to people, predicting and deciding, and implementing and reviewing. The sequence aspect remains the same as stated in Figure 3 and thus a 4 x 5 x 4 tri-dimensional design could be constructed as in Figure 3.

The "social setting" content consists of physical, technological, and human resources, relational systems in the community, the network of organization, and patterns of thought, belief, and value. Process includes continuity and stability, the new and the different, stresses and strains, and resolution and readjustment. Again, the sequence categorization is the same resulting in a 4 x 4 x 4 schematic design.

To summarize this model, then, the job of the administrator is made up of definable content elements. The administrator uses his knowledge about, and understandings of, this content in relation to classifiable administrative functions in a dynamic sequence labeled *time*. The ways in which he performs the administrative functions are determined by his personal capacities and behavior patterns and are affected by the immediate and general social setting in which he is operating.

The staff of the Cooperative Program provided illustrations of how the model worked for them at the end of each section describing the components of the model. Following is an example of a small segment of the discussion by the authors relating to the "man" on the job.

> In sensing problems and gathering appropriate data, the emotional capacity of the *man* is particularly important. One who is willing to ask questions must be secure within his own personal-social environment, so that he will not fear the implications which arise from fuller information. Further, not only must he be willing to ask questions, but he must be emotionally ready and willing to accept the consequences of his inquiry. If a *man* feels threatened by new information, his interpretation of it educationally can scarcely be reliable.[28]

A number of implications might be drawn from this statement in planning educational experiences for administrators. Certainly this would seem to mandate against a "cookbook approach" to training. The educational program should be designed to assist, not hamper, the man in developing an open and unthreatened attitude toward inquiry. The research implications of the statement are even more interesting. A whole series of testable hypotheses are inherent in these four brief sentences.

How has the tri-dimensional concept fared as a beginning in theory development in educational administration? It would seem to have met with mixed success. Training programs for educational administrators have been built across the country employing the assumptions underlying the model. From this point of view, it has certainly had practical utility. It has not, however, stimulated researchers to attempt to validate the model empirically, and few specific research hypotheses have appeared to emerge from the formulation, although, as was illustrated above, there appear to be a number which could be derived from the model. This is probably a result of the basic weakness of the tri-dimensional concept. It is primarily a static classification. The interrelationships of the elements within the three aspects are obtuse, and an attempt was not made to interrelate the aspects.

The tri-dimensional concept, with all its limitations, was a significant effort to organize systematically the diffuse elements of administration. It still stands as a useful illustration of what can be accomplished through model building in administrative theory.

---

[28] *A Developing Concept of the Superintendency in Education*, pp. 17–18.

Administration as decision making. A formal theoretical postulation has purposes quite different from those of the model which was just discussed. The purpose of theory is, of course, not primarily classificatory, but rather explanatory. It must explain the interaction of phenomena in such a way that the future interaction of the phenomena under given conditions are predictable. The theory which will be examined briefly in this section attempts to explain and predict administration in terms of decision making. To provide a base for theoretical development, the following four assumptions were made:

1. There does exist a field of study in administration *qua* administration. Administration is a behavior type to be found in all human organizations.

2. The essence of administration is the control and direction of life in a social organization so that the purposes of the organization are realized and the activities of the organization's members are directed toward that realization.

3. The function of administration in an organization is the effective conduct of the process of decision making—the process through which the administrator exercises the controlling and directing aspects of administration.

4. The administrator reacts and interacts with other individuals in the organization as members of a group, rather than as individuals; that is, the principal reacts to a third-grade student chiefly as a member of the group of third-grade students in his school, rather than to the uniqueness of the student as an individual.

A set of explicit assumptions is a necessary condition for theory development. They are the road signs to the reader that point the direction of the theorizing, its bounds, and cautions to be observed along the way. The reader need not accept all the assumptions before proceeding further in considering the theory, but he cannot interpret the meaning of the theory without knowledge of the assumptions, because the subsequent hypotheses and theorems will be derived from the assumptions used singly and in combination.

In addition to the assumptions underlying the theory, there are concepts which form a base for theory projections. These concepts provide the theorist and the reader with a set of rigorously defined terms and a vantage point from which the next steps in theory building can proceed. In the case of this decision-making theory, the pivotal concept is decision making which is perceived, as will be recalled from the assumptions, as the process of controlling the decision-making process of the organization. Decision making is the process in which the other functions of administration are interpreted. Decision making is defined ". . . to mean not only the decision but also the acts necessary to put the decision in operation."[29] Decisions are also considered as interrelated functions in time; that is, they are sequential rather than terminal.

A variety of other concepts underlying decision-making theory are defined, including organization, communication, power, authority, and perception. To fully appreciate the propositions which follow the assumptions and concepts, the reader would need to be exposed to all the concept definitions, but it is possible to examine one of the major propositions meaningfully if a discussion of the concept of organization is added to those already covered. Organization, then, is defined in relation to its formal and informal aspects —that is, the formal structure which is established explicitly to carry out the decision-making process, and the informal structure which consists of the adaptations of the formal structure made by individuals in the organization in their day-to-day operations to carry out the decision-making function and the goals of the institution as they perceive them.

The next step in theory construction is the statement of explanatory or predictive propositions which are testable logically, analytically, empirically, and experimentally. These propositions should be productive of further propositions and hypotheses which are testable and productive in their turn. The first major proposition in this decision-making theory states:

> *Major proposition.* The structure of an organization is determined by the nature of its decision-making process. The issues of organizational structure such as "span of control" can be resolved if viewed as the outgrowth of a particular type of decision-making process.[30]

This proposition can be examined to illustrate the power of the theory to produce fruitful hypotheses. What should the administrator's span of control be in an organization? This is a problem which has long plagued students of administration, and the answer usually given is that about six persons report to one administrator. This is,

[29] Griffiths, *Administrative Theory,* p. 76.
[30] *Ibid.,* p. 89.

however, the crudest of "rule of thumb" guessing based solely on the attention span of the administrator. The question is unanswerable unless asked in some meaningful framework, and it is suggested here that a meaningful framework be the nature of the decision-making process. Thus, for example, one might hypothesize and test the proposition that an extended span of control (15–25) is more likely to result in decision making close to the point of effective action and consequently to enhance some predetermined measure of organizational effectiveness than is a restricted span of control. Within this context, admitting that the hypothesis requires further operationalizing, the question of what an administrator's span of control needs to be to attain certain organizational decision-making patterns and organizational purposes becomes meaningful.

This theory, of course, requires testing. The heuristic value of the theory has begun to be established as hypotheses are derived from its proposition. The payoff in the testing process is still to come, however. Can the theory predict and explain? Will empirical testing raise telling questions about the nature of the assumptions? Will the propositions hold up or tend to be denied?

As was the case with the tri-dimensional model, it must be reported that no extensive empirical testing has been undertaken on this theory. It does represent another step forward in the process of placing administration on a scientific base, nonetheless, and its significance may be judged in this light even prior to extensive testing.

Summary

The nature of the study of educational administration is progressing from a stage of naked empiricism to a period of scientific inquiry based on administrative theory. This has been a long road of development in a profession that prized the practical man and ridiculed the theorist. The dichotomies of administration—science versus art and practical versus theoretical—seem to have resolved themselves to the point where the integrity of theory and practice is recognized and a science of administration is developing. The implications of theory for the improvement of administrative practice, training, and research have been substantiated by the writings of a number of leading authors in the field.

There are presently existing a variety of theoretical formulations in educational administration employing such diverse bases as role theory, social systems theory, organizational behavior theory, formal organization theory, and the like. Two such formulations were presented and analyzed in this chapter: the tri-dimensional concept of the job of the administrator and a theoretical formulation based on administration as decision making. The next steps in the advancement of administrative theory will require improvement of the taxonomic base of educational administration, more extensive reality testing of existing theories, development of more comprehensive theoretical formulations, and increased communication between theoreticians and practitioners of educational administration.

CHAPTER V

Research in Educational Administration

What is actually known about educational administration? Where has the research in the field led in defining the parameters of the administrator's job and the way in which he should function on the job? Definite answers to such questions are not readily available. From one vantage point it might be reasonable to say that less is known today about administration in education than ever before. With the development of more adequate theory in the field of administration, it is becoming increasingly evident that many things administrators thought they knew several years ago are now not adequate to explain this complex phenomenon called administration. No longer do administrators have explicit faith that the formulas of the scientific managers can be applied to solve all their problems. They do know, however, that such formulas cannot be applied blindly and, in this instance, to know what it is that is not known is a big step forward.

When the substance of school administration dealt with "best practice" solutions to everyday administrative problems, the administrator had the security of a reader of a cookbook in the certainty of the solutions to problems. The research in educational administration was directed toward the refinement of recipes and "tricks of the trade." As Gregg stated in the most recent *Encyclopedia of Educational Research:* "Until a comparatively recent date, research in educational administration was primarily of the historical status, or normative type. This was in harmony with the fact that there were no well-developed theories of administration to give direction to other kinds of research."[1] The status of what is known about educational administration is, then, in a stage of transition. The cookbook phase has been bypassed; the complexity of the operation called administration has been recognized. There is no turning back to a simpler conception of the job, but the out-

---

[1] Russell T. Gregg, "Administration," in *Encyclopedia of Educational Research,* ed. Chester W. Harris (New York: The Macmillan Company, 1960), p. 21.

lines of the knowledge needed by the administrator in the conduct of his work are still only hazily visible. Research has begun to do for administration what it has done for so many other fields of human endeavor. It has made administrators realize how inadequate is their knowledge base, and it has raised more questions than it has answered by providing a glimmer of not only the things not known, but also of the vast new frontiers of knowledge represented by the things which we don't know that we don't know.

A Status Report

The development of research in educational administration is still at a primitive stage. Not only is the research effort quantitatively inadequate, but it is also qualitatively suspect. To understand the nature and patterns of the emergence of new knowledge in this field, it is important for the student of administration to have some clear picture of the amount of research going on, the quality and type of research being produced, and the organized efforts of the profession to affect the quantity and quality of research in the field.

A quantitative analysis. Considered apart from other areas of human endeavor, there may seem to be a considerable amount of activity in research in educational administration. When compared with the research production in other fields, however, this impression dissolves rapidly. For example, in a three year period from 1956–58 studies in school administration compared with the fields of psychology and chemistry as compiled from the *Review of Educational Research, Dissertation Abstracts, Research Studies in America, Chemical Abstracts,* and *Psychological Abstracts* is as follows:[2]

	1956	*1957*	*1958*
Educational Administration	594[a]	594[a]	594[a]
Psychology	8,541	9,074	6,100[b]
Chemistry	105,000	112,000	127,000

[a] Average number of studies in 3 years (total 1,781).
[b] Ten months.

One might conclude from a comparison of these figures that re-

---

[2] Daniel E. Griffiths, *Research in Educational Administration: An Appraisal and a Plan* (New York: Bureau of Publications, Teachers College, Columbia University, 1959), p. 24.

gardless of the quality of the work done in the field of educational administration, this trickle of studies is totally inadequate to serve as the base for rapidly expanding knowledge in any field. Equally as disturbing is the fact that this has been a situation existing for some time. For the twenty-five years prior to 1956, Cooper reports about 15,000 entries on school administration in the *Review of Educational Research,* an average of about 600 a year granting the "not-to-be-taken-for-granted" point that all these entries could be classified reasonably as research studies.[3] As a matter of fact, the assignment of studies and reports as research in the 1956–58 breakdown used more vigorous criteria than simply an entry in the *Review,* so it is likely that the 1,781 studies reported in these three years represent an increasing tempo of research activity in the late 1950's as contrasted with earlier years. Without belaboring the point further, however, let it be stated simply that there has been a dearth of research activity in school administration for many years. The scarcity continues to the present, despite a discernible gradual and upward trend in quantitative adequacy.

Qualitative analysis. There is substantial evidence that the quality of the research endeavor in school administration has left something to be desired. The emphasis in the selection of problem areas for study has clearly been placed on the technical aspects of administration—salary scheduling, budgeting, pupil and class scheduling, housekeeping, and so forth. The research has been static rather than dynamic. Researchers in the field have tended to be mesmerized by routine surveys of "best" administrative practices. Experimental and descriptive investigations directed toward the development of explanatory theory have been few and far between. The field has been plagued by the ills of educational research in general in terms of inadequate research designs and patterns of analysis.

A number of reasons could be brought forth for this discouraging picture of the quality of research in the field. One of the first to be identified would certainly be the minimal programs of research training in educational administration available at most institutions. It might reasonably be contended that the inherent conflict between the personality of the administrator (the man of action) and the

---

[3] Dan H. Cooper, "School Administration," *Review of Educational Research,* XXVI, No. 3 (1956), p. 211.

researcher (the reflective thinker) has made it difficult to attract researchers to train themselves for work in this field. There is little doubt that research has not been highly valued by the educational administrator, and this has probably contributed to the deficiencies in the state of the art.

There are, too, less obvious reasons that can be brought forth. The research in the field has been responsive to the immediate problems faced by the practitioner—so responsive, in fact, that the kinds of questions asked have been posed in the language of the practitioner rather than the language of the researcher. For example, the school administrator must certainly make a decision in regard to the class size which he will maintain in his school or school district; but it is not true, as seems to have been assumed, that the researcher can make that decision for him. Research can provide evidence on the impact of certain size classes, on pupils with certain characteristics who are pursuing defined activities in relation to particular desired outcomes; but the administrator's decision is not compelled in a single direction by this evidence. He must still weigh the evidence with his board of education in relation to the kinds of factors affecting administration which were described earlier in this book. The advantage of a particular class size for gifted students will have to be assessed against other equally pressing or more pressing demands for another type of service. The search for a single "best class size" forces the researcher into the position of the alchemist, and this is the position which has too often been accepted by researchers in educational administration.

The exhorters and affirmers must also assume responsibility for the questionable status of research in this field. Too many of the few research resources available have been devoted to an attempt to substantiate positions or policies already assumed to be desirable. The literature is replete with efforts to "study" decisions already arrived at so that those who question the decisions can be quieted. Class size studies again afford a good example. Administrators assumed from their own experience in the classroom and from the comments reported by their teachers that small classes represented better educational situations than large classes. They sold this conclusion to their boards of education who, in turn, began to question the conclusion when they faced fiscal difficulties in the school district. Evidence was needed to support the decision and it needed to be unequivocal. Studies by the hundreds, with mixed results, were mounted to answer the need. New knowledge was neither sought nor found, but the energies of scores of researchers were diverted to the effort.

In summary, a statement by the late Tom Lamke, in his analysis of the qualitative problems of research in teacher personnel, bears repeating:

> If the research during the last three years were to be wiped out in the fields of medicine, agriculture, physics, or chemistry, our lives would be materially changed. If research in the area of teacher personnel during the last three years should vanish, education and educators would continue much as usual. There are relatively few studies among the some 500 reported here which will, or should, widely affect educational practice.[4]

It is sad but true to note that most serious researchers analyzing the work in the field of educational administration would make the same statement as Lamke has made about the closely related field of teacher personnel. Administrative research has not reached that level of maturity where the work being done is critically important to the development of the field. Of the some 600–700 studies done each year, a very few are of enduring significance.

Forces of change. On the positive side of the ledger (as was noted in the discussion of administrative theory in the last chapter) the picture has been changing for the past several years. Two events which occurred just before the beginning of the decade of the 1950's influenced profoundly the direction which research in the field of educational administration was to follow. The W. K. Kellogg Foundation decided to support the improvement of the field of school administration, and the leading professors in the field established an effective organization called the National Conference of Professors of Educational Administration. The Kellogg Foundation's interest in the field culminated in the establishment of eight centers to study the field of educational administration under the title Cooperative Program in Educational Administration. Stimulated by the work of these centers, and benefitting from the time available to professors to pursue their field in a scholarly

---

[4] Tom A. Lamke, "Introduction," *Review of Educational Research*, XXV, No. 3 (1955), p. 192.

fashion, the CPEA developed into an organization in which research could be discussed, analyzed, and planned.

By the end of the 1950's, the CPEA had become a permanent fixture in school administration through the establishment of the University Council for Educational Administration, an organization devoted to the improvement of preparation programs in educational administration and the conduct of research in the field through interuniversity cooperation. The simultaneous emergence of a number of sources of support for the conduct of research in school administration—for example, the Cooperative Research Program of the United States Office of Education—provided the final ingredient to a renewed impetus toward research development in the field.

These forces of change have had a significant impact on research in educational administration. The emergence of theoretical formulations was noted in the last chapter, and with the development of these new rubrics for use in research many investigators have been freed to move beyond the stage of normative and historical studies. A new body of content has been emerging in school administration, indicating that the earlier cited quotation from Lamke may not be characteristic of research in educational administration in the future.

What is Being Learned

The way in which knowledge is organized in a field often provides important clues to the type of research being conducted and the knowledge base on which the practitioner is acting. In reviewing the reports on research in school administration which appeared in the *Review of Educational Research* during its first twenty-five years, Cooper noted that the way in which the structure of administration was viewed has undergone substantial change. He reported seven categories which he felt represented the order of dominance of particular knowledge blocks as they developed in the field. They were as follows:

I. Categories of Educational Level:
>Nursery and Kindergarten; Elementary Education; Secondary Education.
II. Categories of Technical Administration:
>Organization within the Structure of Government; District

Organization; Organization of Administrative Hierarchy; Instructional Organization; Employed Personnel; Finance and Business Administration; School Plant and Equipment; Pupil Services; School and Community Relationships.

III. Categories of Governmental Level:
   Federal; State; Intermediate District; Local.
IV. Categories of Rural-Urban School Administration.
V. Categories of Public-Private School Administration.
VI. Categories of Role and Behavior:
   Preparation; Personality; Personal Relationships.
VII. Categories of Time-Sequence:
   Establishing Purposes; Making Plans; Executing Plans; Evaluating Results.
VIII. Methodologies and Mechanisms for Administrative Research.[5]

This is not intended to represent a hierarchy of values in terms of what is important in administration. Older topics have not been supplanted; they have been supplemented and, of course, it is quite possible to classify and then discuss the same piece of research under several of the above-named categories.

There is, however, a significance in this changing classification system of knowledge. Category I was more important as a vantage point for viewing administration, for example, when little attention was paid to the common elements of administration as a science. It tends to emphasize such topics as scheduling in the secondary school as a function discrete from elementary school administration, where the problem does not exist in the same form. Categories II–V illustrate topics which are particularly susceptible to investigation through status and normative studies; these categories clearly emphasize the form, rather than the substance, of administration. Categories VI–VII are less open to investigation employing traditional survey techniques; they impel the adoption of more diverse research tools from related social and behavioral sciences.

The concentration in the remainder of this chapter will be on these latter topical areas, not because the field is standing still in relation to knowledge about the form of administration, but because the unique features of what is being learned now, as contrasted with earlier research efforts in school administration, lie in

---

[5] Dan H. Cooper, "School Administration," *Review of Educational Research,* XXVI, No. 3 (1956), p. 212.

these latter categories which emphasize the process and function of administration.

Organizational behavior. A provocative area of new knowledge is growing up around a traditional topic, organization, which has taken on new coloration. Instead of the limited notion of organization considered as a technical administrative function, or, even more commonly, considered as a description of intergovernmental relations, organization is being examined as a behavioral phenomenon. In the 1961 *Review of Educational Research* issue on "Educational Organization, Administration, and Finance," Campbell and Faber cited fifteen examples of research studies and theoretical formulations completed in the preceding three years which related directly to this topic.[6]

This research is providing a new vantage point from which the administrator can study his operations. For example, Argyris has investigated what he hypothesizes as an inherent conflict between self-realization for the individual and the attainment of institutional goals. He proposes the recognition of this conflict as an operating dimension of the institution, rather than diminution of attention to a real conflict situation by pretending that extrinsic rewards and motivations can overcome the nature of the conflict.[7]

The concept that institutions or organizations can be studied from a behavioral reference point, rather than accepted as inert constants in the study of administration, has been made possible by such formulations as those of March and Simon (in which the organization is seen as a unit composed of series of subunits represented by individuals as decision makers and problem solvers)[8] and of Carlson (who views the dynamics of organizational behavior in terms of social systems theory, with a consequent postulation of the internal and external sanctions which influence the behavior of the organization).[9]

This body of emerging new knowledge equips the administrator,

---

[6] Roald F. Campbell and Charles F. Faber, "Administrative Behavior: Theory and Research," *Review of Educational Research,* XXXI, No. 4 (1961), pp. 355–58.

[7] Chris Argyris, *Personality and Organization* (New York: Harper & Row, Publishers, 1957).

[8] James G. March and Herbert A. Simon, *Organizations* (New York: John Wiley & Sons, Inc., 1958).

[9] R. O. Carlson, "Research and the School System as an Organization," *School Review,* 66, No. 3 (1958), pp. 473–83.

as he has never been equipped in the past, with an understanding of the dynamics of the situation in which he finds himself. Hopefully, of course, this understanding may lead him to different and more effective bases for decision making about the form and functions of his organization.

Administrative roles. How does the classroom teacher perceive the role of the building principal? Conversely, how does the principal perceive the role of the classroom teacher? Does it make a difference if the perceptions of the teacher and the administrator differ? It most emphatically does, and this illustrates another body of information which has burgeoned during the past ten years. Bidwell reported that teachers who were dissatisfied felt that, on the one hand, they were unable to predict what the administrator would do in any given situation and, on the other hand, they could not determine what it was that the administrator expected of them. In the same study, satisfied teachers trusted their impressions of what the administrators were supposed to be doing and how they would do it and felt that they knew what the administrators expected of them.[10] Here were two groups of individuals toward whom the administrator could act identically and still expect completely different reactions. The situation proves to be an anomaly only if the administrator is unfamiliar with the application of role theory to the study of administration.

The first extensive report on administrative roles in education appeared in the *Review of Educational Research,* October, 1955, but all issues since that time have given attention to this expanding field of knowledge. Role studies have now been conducted covering a wide variety of aspects of administration and administrative positions, including the roles played by the superintendent in working with the community; role expectations of teachers, citizens, board members, and parents; those of the positions of principal, superintendent, and curriculum director; personal role perceptions held by superintendents, principals, and teachers; role conflicts experienced by various administrators in their positions, as well as role conflicts among administrators filling different positions; and, perhaps most elaborately, Getzels and Guba postulated the concept of a school as a social system, with the effectiveness of the individual in the

---

[10] Charles E. Bidwell, "Some Causes of Conflicts and Tensions Among Teachers," *Administrator's Notebook,* IV, No. 7 (1952), pp. 1–4.

system being determined by his behavior relative to the expectation of his behavior held by others.[11]

The application of role theory to a more adequate understanding of the process of administration has already reaped high rewards and is likely to continue to form the base for the addition of new knowledge in the field.

Administrative leadership. Leadership is, of course, hardly a new term in the field of educational administration. For years, the administrator has been exhorted to exercise leadership in his position. The problem has been that the concept of leadership was so nebulous that the administrator was at a loss to respond to the exhortations. Recently, investigations of leader behavior in organizations and small groups have added concrete dimensions to the term.

Several of the works already mentioned in this chapter have contributed to an understanding of the phenomenon of leadership in organizations. For example, the Getzels-Guba model introduced to school administration the concept of varying leadership styles related to varying role perceptions held by the administrator. They classified leader behavior into three categories. The nomothetic leader was one who stressed conformity of role behavior to institutional goals. The idiographic leader emphasized the individual and minimized the press of the institution on the individual's role. The transactional leader assumed an intermediate position in the resolution of the individual-institutional conflict.[12] This notion of classifiable, identifiable leader-behavior styles provides a base for discussion and, more importantly, for investigation of the phenomenon of leadership.

In summarizing what has been learned about group leadership in recent years, Ramseyer includes such propositions as the following which indicate the reduction of the general concept to operational terms for study:

> Leadership is a product of the interaction which takes place among individuals in a group, not of the status or position of these individuals.
> Because a person exhibits leader behavior in one group is no

---

[11] Jacob W. Getzels and Egon G. Guba, "Social Behavior and the Administrative Process," *School Review*, 65, No. 4 (1957), pp. 423–41.

[12] *Ibid.*, pp. 423–41.

guarantee that he will or can do so in others. All people exhibit this behavior in some degree in certain groups.

Status assignments may either enhance or reduce the effectiveness of leader behavior. Such assignments place individuals in group situations where this behavior is more readily perceived by greater numbers of people. Status (if used as power) may destroy the effectiveness of leader behavior.

The leader does not determine the norms of the group; groups choose, as leaders, the persons who best exemplify their norms. Every group has certain critical norms which the leader must exemplify.

The effectiveness of leader behavior is measured in terms of mutuality of goals, productivity in the achievement of these goals, and the maintenance of group solidarity.[13]

Illustrating the emerging new knowledge on leadership at a more specific level, one can turn to the studies of perceptions of leader behavior. Using a device called the Leadership Behavior Description Questionnaire, Halpin investigated the criteria being applied to the evaluation of leadership by both leaders and subordinates. One of the conflicts identified by Halpin was the opposite evaluations of supervisors and subordinates regarding the contributions of the dimensions of consideration and initiating structure to effective leadership. He felt that this represented a basic dilemma faced by the administrator in exercising his leadership function.[14] Interestingly enough, a subsequent study using a different sample of administrators (principals, rather than superintendents or aircraft commanders) showed agreement between principals and teachers on the need for strong behavior on the part of the principal in these two dimensions.[15] Further investigation of the impact of administrative distance on superior-subordinate reactions to the LBDQ would appear to be called for to clarify the nature of the differences already discovered.

A number of other variables affecting leadership behavior have been investigated, including such elements as patterns of commu-

[13] John A. Ramseyer, "A Concept of Educational Leadership," in *Leadership for Improving Instruction* (Washington, D.C.: Association for Supervision and Curriculum Development, 1960), pp. 56–57.

[14] Andrew W. Halpin, "The Leadership Behavior and Combat Performance of Airplane Commanders," *Journal of Abnormal and Social Psychology*, 49, No. 1 (1954), pp. 19–22.

[15] Warren L. Evenson, "Leadership Behavior of High School Principals," *Bulletin of the National Association of Secondary-School Principals*, 43, No. 248 (1959), pp. 96–101.

nication within the institution, general level of morale, and the value structures of superiors and subordinates. The addition of each of these variables tends to explain another piece of the mosaic which is leader behavior. For example, when values were added for investigation, it became apparent that the teacher's perception of the principal as an effective or ineffective leader was related closely to the extent to which the administrator and teacher shared a common value system. Teachers rated as ineffective those principals whose value systems differed from theirs. But the converse was not true. Differences in values held seemed to have no relationship to the principal's rating of the teacher as effective or ineffective.[16]

Today's school administrator need not rely on a vague feeling that he should exercise leadership without understanding what leadership is or what reaction he can expect from subordinates when he does attempt to exhibit such behavior. At least a base of knowledge has been developed on which he can act with intelligence and purpose.

Community impact on school administration. The topic of the community's impact on school administration is included for a very particular reason: It is representative of a change in research emphasis within a traditional category. If one refers again to the Cooper outline of topics included in the *Review* over the years, one will note that "school and community relationships" are not in the newer category at all; they are a time-honored subdivision of the "technical administration" category. An analysis of textbooks in educational administration will reveal the same fact. The studies of the past few years, however, have moved so rapidly from the traditional treatment of the topic as a primer in public relations for the school superintendent, to an interdisciplinary study of the dynamics of the interaction of the school and the community, that the traditional topic is hardly recognizable in its new garb.

With school districts across the country caught in a fiscal squeeze (see Chapter II), the Stanford Institute for Communication Research undertook a national analysis of the responses of voters to their schools. For the first time, voter attitudes toward schools were identified, categorized, and analyzed, and a systematic body of knowledge is emerging to explain the often confusing patterns

---

[16] Richard Prince, "Individual Values and Administrative Effectiveness," *Administrator's Notebook,* 6, No. 4 (1957), pp. 1–4.

of results obtained when a school district seeks community support for the construction of new schools or the establishment of higher budgets. Anyone who proceeded through an educational administration training program ten years ago will recall the platitudes about providing information to all citizens about their schools preparatory to a voter issue on the schools. The assumption underlying this exhorting was clearly that the citizens were generally informed about, and sympathetic to, education and that they needed a little extra boost in times of crisis. The fact of the matter, however, seems to be that the majority have little or no information about the schools, in many cases are not at all disturbed about their ignorance, and in all cases can be distinguished differentially by sex, age, family, and economic status in terms of the kinds of information they need and want and the effect they are likely to have on the outcome of the election if they are encouraged to participate.[17]

Political scientists, economists, sociologists, social psychologists, anthropologists, and communications analysts have all contributed to this new flavor of knowledge regarding the community and the work of the school administrator. The nature of the power structure in communities, the ways in which they are likely to affect the operation of the schools, the values various subgroups of the citizenry hold toward education, the effect of mass media on the formulation of opinions toward education by the citizenry, the effects of urbanization on the relationship of the community to the schools, the communications systems which exist in the community, and the dynamics of the competition for the tax dollar have all been subjected to intensive study in recent years.

The well-informed school administrator must now consider knowledge about the community to be a part of the substance of educational administration—not merely intuitive knowledge about his own community, but systematic knowledge about communities as an interdisciplinary phenomenon of the culture in which the schools must live and grow.

Mechanisms for administrative research. It is not quite fair to categorize this topic with the previous four which have been discussed. It does not represent what we know about administration, but it is an element of what is being learned. Leaders in educational administration have discovered that new knowledge for and about

---

[17] Richard R. Carter, *Voters and Their Schools* (Stanford, Calif.: Institute for Communication Research, 1960).

their field of specialization will not just grow—it needs cultivation. A recent publication on research in educational administration faces this issue squarely and devotes itself almost exclusively to the social and institutional factors affecting research in educational administration, the methodological considerations of research in this field, and the recruitment, training, and development of researchers in educational administration.[18]

Undoubtedly, the last decade has seen the establishment of mechanisms of financial support and moral stimulation for administrative research in education. School administration has been influenced profoundly by the addition of the skills of social and behavioral scientists to the study of educational problems, and the adoption of many of the techniques of these allied disciplines has opened new vistas to educational investigators. An attempt was made to try to convey some of the flavor of this renaissance of interest in research in administration in the last chapter on theory and in the earlier part of this chapter when the history of the new movement was reviewed in greater detail. The best method for doing this, however, may be through a case study of one project which sprang directly from the new mechanisms for research. In the next section, then, a single research project will be reviewed. This was the first effort in which the University Council for Educational Administration was able to exhibit its ability to sustain an interinstitutional investigation through the cooperation of a number of its member institutions. The subject matter of the investigation is administrative behavior, a topic which is characteristic of the newer emphasis in educational administration. The techniques employed in the study are unique in the field of educational administration and reflect a heavy interdisciplinary orientation. This is truly an example of modern research in school administration.

A Case in Point[19]

The study being reported here was called the DCS Project, mean-

---

18 Jack A. Culbertson and Stephen P. Hencley, eds., *Educational Research: New Perspectives* (Danville, Ill.: the Interstate Printers and Publishers, Inc., 1963).

19 The material presented in this section is summarized from John K. Hemphill, Daniel E. Griffiths, and Norman Frederiksen, *Administrative Performance and Personality* (New York: Bureau of Publications, Teachers College, Columbia University, 1962).

ing the Development of Criteria of Success in School Administration Project. The primary objective of the research was "to
determine dimensions of performance in the elementary school
principalship and thus to develop a better understanding of the job
of the school administrator."[20] The general research strategy to attain this objective was a marked departure from previous efforts in
the field. Up to this time, the principal source of data on the performance of educational administrators was either a questionnaire
survey or interview with practicing administrators who reported
what they did on the job (with all the obvious hazards and unre-
liability which one might expect from the technique) and a few
instances of isolated observation of how a school administrator
went about his work. The research team on this study undertook
the construction of a simulated school situation building on the "in-
basket" technique which had been developed by one of the investigators, Frederiksen, for studying the administrative behavior of
Air Force officers.

This process of simulation resulted in the construction of a standard administrative situation called the Whitman School.[21] In a
number of testing centers around the country, 232 elementary
school principals became the principal of the Whitman School and,
additionally, submitted to a variety of tests of ability, knowledge,
interest, and personality. To complete the data gathering, information was obtained on the principal's experience and training.

This vast quantity of data, exceeding by far any previous accumulation of information on educational administrative behavior,
was made possible by the adoption of the simulation technique. Its
analysis was made possible by the application of modern statistical
methods and the availability of computers to process the data. The
investigators were working in an area in which the research of
school administration has been particularly barren despite repeated
attempts to gather data: the analysis of administrative behavior and
the correlation of the differences in behavior with differential personal and background characteristics. The repeated failure of the
"trait approach" to provide such data is a classic example of the

---

[20] *Ibid.*, p. 7.
[21] Readers who are interested in the details of the simulated situation and the
way in which it was administered are referred to Hemphill, Griffiths, and Frederiksen, *op. cit.*, pp. 17–62.

frustration of research. The results of this study, however, justified the investigation beyond the hopes of its most enthusiastic supporters. A few of the findings and implications will be presented in the following paragraphs.

Findings—selection. Who will make a good school principal? That, of course, depends upon what you think a good principal is, but the DCS Project provides information on how your candidate will perform his administrative tasks and you can decide whether or not that is "good" in your own terms. Should you, for example, select a woman for a school administrative post? Prejudice in the field would definitely indicate that you should not. The DCS data indicate, ". . . that as a class men are not overwhelmingly superior to women as elementary school principals. The evidence appears to favor women if the job of the principal is conceived in a way that values working with teachers and outsiders; being concerned with objectives of teaching, pupil participation, and the evaluation of learning; having knowledge of teaching methods and techniques; and gaining positive reactions from teachers and superiors. But the relationship is not so strong that choosing a woman will automatically produce these characteristics; there is a great deal of overlapping of the distributions of scores on such attributes."[22]

How about experience? The evidence is not as clear-cut as one might assume it would be from checking certification standards. "Those principals who have little administrative experience tend to follow suggestions made by others and to discuss with others before taking final action. Those with more administrative experience respond to outsiders, direct the work of others, and analyze the situation."[23] There seemed to be little difference between the two groups on the crucial question of providing direction to the instructional program.

Interesting differences did appear on the personality and interest measures, and the project staff suggested that ". . . personality and interest tests might profitably be employed after all candidates have been screened for mental ability and professional and general knowledge."[24] These latter tests differentiated favorably for high

---

[22] *Ibid.,* p. 334.
[23] *Ibid.,* p. 335.
[24] *Ibid.,* pp. 339–40.

scores on a variety of dimensions including the relatively crucial one of high work output.

Findings—practice of administration. By identifying a number of behavior categories which were seldom used by the principals in the simulated situation, the project staff uncovered a number of surprises and a few affirmations of commonly held opinions about educational administrative behavior. The school appeared to be ". . . a highly formal organization with strong authority orientation."[25] The principals, in carrying out their tasks, seldom employed the available categories of "Informality to Outsiders" and "Informality to Superiors."

Quite surprisingly, the principals did not appear to exhibit behavior which might be classified as improving or backing up their staffs. Instead, they seemed to substitute a kind of formal courtesy for vigorous support and interest in the welfare of their staff. The researchers concluded: "While this lack of concern may be an artifact of the simulation, the lack is so nearly complete that it does not seem as though this is the only reason."[26]

The categories of delegation indicated that almost no delegation occurs in a typical elementary school which conflicts with the encouragement to principals on the part of professors and texts in school administration to attempt to delegate more of their responsibilities. As the investigators pointed out, however, in the typical elementary school there is no one to whom the principal might delegate responsibility except the teachers, and they already have full-time jobs.

Perhaps the most interesting single finding on administrative practices relates to the housekeeping details of the school. For years the elementary school principal has been belabored with the accusation that he is so tied up with the housekeeping affairs of his school that he fails to provide leadership and attention to the instructional program. This did not appear to be the case. The principals seldom employed the categories relating to physical values and the researchers concluded: "It would appear that the stereotype of the elementary school principal as a 'housekeeper' is not justified in terms of the findings of this study."[27]

---

[25] *Ibid.*, p. 346.
[26] *Ibid.*, p. 346.
[27] *Ibid.*, p. 347.

Summary. This study is an excellent example of the new frontier in research in educational administration. The results of the research added a whole body of new knowledge to the substance of what we know about the practice of administration in education. Equally as important, the investigation opened a fascinating series of follow-up studies which can build on the research already completed. The study results and the simulated technique employed in the project have already influenced most preparation programs for school administrators in this country and in Canada.

During the next few years the profession of educational administration can look forward hopefully to a multiplicity of such studies which, while employing the techniques and knowledge of the social and behavioral sciences, will take advantage of the mechanisms now available for research in educational administration to establish a significant body of independent researchers and new knowledge for school administration.

The Steps Ahead

There is an old and respected game played in educational circles which results in long lists of research priorities. The object of the game is somewhat obscure, however, because no researchers ever refer to the lists. In looking ahead at the next steps in research in educational administration, we will not play that game, assuming that the essence of basic research is "not knowing what you don't know." Instead, an attempt will be made to summarize the years ahead in research in educational administration as seen by the editors of chapters on school administration research in the *Review of Educational Research* during the past six years.

Several of the authors noted the trend toward theory-based research and conjectured that this trend will continue and will provide a more satisfactory base for the projection of significant findings. Attention was called to the fact that there was a continuing overemphasis on status and descriptive studies, but all the authors who reported this felt that the condition was improving and that future efforts would not be restricted to such static designs. Recognition was given to a generally more favorable climate for research development, including not only the availability of more funds to support research endeavors, but also a more vigorous interest in research in educational administration on the part of associated professional organizations. Repeated attention was drawn to the broader base from which administrative research in education is proceeding with the employment of interdisciplinary techniques and knowledge drawn especially from the fields of sociology and psychology. The failure to use terms to connote concepts with any degree of consistency among various research studies is a nagging problem which will undoubtedly place emphasis on taxonomic and classificatory problems in the upcoming years. The over-all prognosis seemed to be favorable, summarized well by the following statement from Griffiths and Iannaccone:

> One has the feeling that research in educational administration is coming to life. As researchers, the reviewers have the feeling that this is a good time in which to live. We are in transition, we have many unsolved problems, but we are vigorous, and we are pointed in a direction which cannot help but be productive.[28]

Summary

Until recent years, research in educational administration has tended to emphasize status studies of the technical aspects of administration. The research effort has been deficient in both quantity and quality to provide a dynamic base for the training of administrative practitioners.

A number of organizations in school administration have worked together to change this picture. Current studies are beginning to emphasize experimental methodologies and to investigate such areas as organizational behavior, administrative roles, administrative leadership, and the interrelationships of the school and its social setting.

A case study was presented of a modern research project in educational administration which employed interdisciplinary research techniques to penetrate a previously obscure area of knowledge in school administration. The look ahead toward the development of new knowledge about educational administration appears promising.

---

[28] Daniel E. Griffiths and Laurence Iannaccone, "Administrative Theory, Relationships, and Preparation," *Review of Educational Research*, XXVIII, No. 4 (1958), p. 334.

CHAPTER VI

A Look to the Future

A discussion of educational administration would be incomplete and inadequate without reference to what the future may hold for administrators, boards of education, and school systems. Materials in each of the preceding chapters have provided cues to upcoming changes in administration and in some instances have predicted what can be expected. In this chapter, we will concentrate on the future and project (with a cloudy crystal ball) some of the factors and concerns that will shape educational administration in the years ahead.

There are at least three levels of prognostication possible, and the element of risk in the predictions increases as one moves from one to the other. The first might be designated as trends in administration. At this level the predictor is on fairly sound ground. For example, the total number of school districts has decreased in number from 127,649 in 1932 to 36,402 in 1961, and this development of fewer and larger school-district units shows no sign of abatement.[1] This will undoubtedly affect the character of school administration in the years ahead and is not difficult or precarious to predict.

A second level, which might be termed emerging developments, includes those changes which have just begun to take hold but which appear to have staying power. In this category, for example, might be included a development such as the professionalization of school administration which has begun to emerge in the last few years through the efforts of such organizations as the American Association of School Administrators.

The third category consists of changes which have hardly begun to take shape but which can be derived from current conditions and indications. For example, it is quite apparent that school systems

---

[1] William J. Ellena and Robert M. Isenberg, *School District Organization: Journey That Must Not End* (Washington, D.C.: The American Association of School Administrators, 1962), p. 1.

have long been relatively unresponsive institutions to needed reform and change. Changes that have taken place have been additive and refining in nature, but not through redefinition. One could predict that this situation will not be tolerated by the patrons of the schools and the profession itself in the future. If it is not, basic structural changes will be required to facilitate redefinitions and changes in school districts. The nature of these changes may take several forms, and the predictor is clearly operating at the "best guess" level in selecting the pattern most likely to emerge and persist.

Despite the inherent dangers in the art of prediction, the authors would like to do their best in charting briefly the confrontations that will determine the shape of administration in the future, as they see it, at each of these levels.

Trends in Administration

This topic has been treated in the previous chapters and only a brief recapitulation will be attempted here. Many of the problems to be faced by educational administration in the future will be occasioned by population increases; additions to knowledge; new forms of energy; the posture of this nation in the world community; the rise of new nations, technology, and automation; and worldwide rivalry of ideologies. Some resultant specific trend determiners which are affecting administration are size factors in administrative units, urbanization and finance, increasing demands upon the schools, population problems and automation.

Size considerations. Ironically, size has a two-way implication for shaping the future of educational administration. Although the number of school districts in each state has been reduced drastically, the number must be still further reduced to form defensible and efficient administrative units. On the other hand, large metropolitan school districts will be continually in search for ways and means for effective decentralization of operations to maximize local autonomy and obviate many of the difficulties related to bigness.

Changes involved in either situation have administrative implications for organization, communication, public relations, programming, staffing, and educational statesmanship. The governing criterion will be an organization which fosters maximal educational and economic efficiency while maintaining the strongest possible local autonomy and self-contained independence in operations. This envisions new concepts in district central office organization as well as a more responsible and comprehensive staffing at the operational unit level.

Urbanization. Educational administration will have no choice in the matter of whether or not it must adjust in the future to urbanization and the complexity that goes with it. The trend of urbanization already noted in the more populous regions of the nation will continue unabated, due not alone to the increasing population, but to the nature of living requirements in an industrialized economy and society.

The implications for administration of urbanization were mentioned in Chapter II. The point of emphasis here is that the trend toward urbanization will make the "Centerville Case" a normal expectancy to which administration must adjust and function, not only as such communities develop, but also as they continue to exist, stabilize, and mature.

Fiscal developments. It is the contention of the authors that the trend toward improvement of the quality of education will be accelerated on the bases of "command performance" on the part of constituents and on the pressure of international competition and survival. New definitions of educational programs, extensions of education to meet needs of many segments of society, continued emphasis on technical and scientific programs, and the like will increase cost factors.

Parallel trends in demands for all kinds of governmental and municipal services will place education in a continually more competitive position for revenues. The implications are obvious— stronger demands for economics, better efficiency and defense of expenditures for education, and increasing difficulties on all levels in obtaining adequate financial appropriations. Experiences in state legislatures dealing with appropriations for education and the records of local levies and referendums for education underscore the significance of this factor as an item to be reckoned with in the future of educational administration.

Extension of services. The trend in education has been to assume an increasing burden of responsibilities—transportation, recreation, food services, health services, and the like. Of course, many of these services are directly related to education, but some seemed to be acquired by the school system largely because it is the one organized public agency in the community available to turn to for service. Whether the schools have overextended themselves in this regard is not for the authors to decide. This trend of continued extension of services by the schools, however, is a factor having serious implications on the shaping of administrative problems in the future.

How far the local school system can and should go in the direction of providing extended services is a question that must be coped with. Who should assume responsibility for upward and downward extension of educational programs, adult education, technical training, retraining programs, and the like? What assistance will be made available to the local districts in assuming these new roles and responsibilities?

Mobility of population. Every indication points to increasing mobility of population in an increasingly complex technological culture and an industrialized society. The trend is likely not to be reversed. People follow opportunities. Census and demographic data provide ample evidence of the dimensions of population shifts and changes.

The implications of this phenomenon for educational administration are twofold: (1) the effect of mobility on the educational program and efforts to meet the needs of both the stable and mobile segments of the school population; and (2) the practical aspects of dealing with and obtaining necessary support and commitment to the educational enterprise in a transient society. Communication is just one problem generated by mobility and transiency. It is readily seen that establishing and maintaining communication in situations of extreme turnover and change in population creates serious problems.

Automation and cybernation. The trend toward automation and cybernation becomes more visible daily. To think of these phenomena as merely a final stage in the evolution of technological labor-saving grossly underrates their importance and potential impact upon labor, management, and society. Taken together, automated devices and computer systems not only may replace and improve on many human capacities to perform, but may perform complex logical and decision-making functions.

The implications of automation and cybernation to education and to educational administration are so manifold that they defy analysis and description here. Automatic data processing has already had wide acceptance in school administration—census, scheduling, accounting, programming, inventory controls, payroll, personnel data, analysis, and the like. Some of the advantages claimed for automation are that it (1) reduces personnel needed in operations, which reduces the magnitude of management's human relations tasks, human error, and other labor-management problems; (2) steps up efficiency factors; (3) permits much greater rationalization of managerial activities; frees management of petty distractions and provides time and opportunity for major decision making; and (4) provides whole new concepts in coordination, controls, dispersal of operations and the like.[2]

In brief, the impact of automation on educational administration is twofold: first, in the adoption and utilization of automation and cybernation in the operations of the educational enterprise; and second, in the educational and societal consequences of the trend which ultimately will be reflected redefinition of the entire educational program and process.

Emerging Developments

Throughout the preceding chapters allusions have been made regarding emerging developments—phenomena not quite substantiable as trends, yet possible precursors to trends in developmental stages. While these are too numerous to delineate in detail, a few which appear to have potential implications for educational administration are noted in the following paragraphs.

Professionalization of the administrator. Minimal characteristics of a profession include a definite specialized body of knowledge and skills, a prescribed preservice preparation program, legal sanction for practitioners, an ethical code, and a system of self-policing by members in the profession. Advanced professions have instituted professional standards, specific requirements in preservice and in-service training, accreditation of training institutions, professional organization at state and national levels, and cooperative involvement of practitioners in research, contributing to professional literature and preparation programs.

---

[2] See Donald N. Micheal, *Cybernation: The Silent Conquest* (Santa Barbara, Calif.: Center for the Study of Democratic Institutions, 1962).

The will to become more professionalized has been exhibited by school administrators in many ways. An example is the effort put forth by the American Association of School Administrators in 1961, when it passed an amendment to its constitution providing that "beginning January 1, 1964, all new members of the Association shall submit evidence of successful completion of two (2) years of graduate study in university programs designed to prepare school administrators and approved by an accreditation body endorsed by the Executive Committee of the Association." In addition, the Association inaugurated a Committee for the Advancement of the Superintendency in the Association (CASA). A yearbook of the Association was dedicated to a study of the superintendency.[3]

A special commission of the association published a monumental report in 1963 again pointing up the needs for more rigor and posture in preservice and in-service growth and development of the membership.[4] State administrator organizations have become interested and involved in the promotion of certification requirements, cooperation with training institutions, better recruitment and screening practices, research, internship practices, and preparation programs. The implications of all this to educational administration seem clear: Administrators of the future will be better prepared, more carefully selected, and more competent professionally to execute their responsibilities.

Extension of knowledge. The emerging interest in research on administration and on many facets of education is providing a body of new knowledge for educators and administrators that holds much promise for the future. The reader is urged to review Chapters IV and V as a basis for perceiving the implications of research and the extension of knowledge for educational administration. The authors believe that the activity and interest in research and new knowledge about administration mark the threshold of a trend which will have far-reaching effects on shaping the future of educational administration.

Media of communication. Another harbinger of the future for administration lies in the new and imaginative use of media for

---

[3] *Professional Administrators For America's Schools* (Washington, D.C.: American Association of School Administrators, 1960).

[4] *In-service Education for School Administration* (Washington, D.C.: American Association of School Administrators, 1963).

communication and instruction. Radio, television, video tapes, re-corders, language laboratories, sound film, and similar media have gained general acceptance in educational systems. Two-way per-sonal television communication between the administrator and the parent is a likely possibility, or a similar contact with the entire community.

The dire need to establish and maintain communication between home and school in an increasingly complex societal situation em-phasizes the need for maximal utilization of all media available. More use of communications media in educational administration is a potential trend worthy of serious consideration.

Curricular developments. The inevitability of change in pro-grams of education to meet the needs of the future requires no documentation; it is a reality to which educational administration must continually address itself. Indeed, program and staffing are probably the two most knotty problems to be faced in the future of school operations. It is the problem of what should be taught, to whom, when, how and by whom.

What will emerge from the new knowledges to be taught? How will the local schools relate to the new programs in science, mathe-matics, English, and other subjects? For instance, will the Physical Science Study Committee program in physics and the School Mathe-matics Study Group program in mathematics, to name two, become the nationally accepted programs for schools? Shall we have a national curriculum?

Without commenting on the merits of the situation, the indica-tions are that local school administrations will be called upon to decide whether or not their schools want to conform to nationally accepted norms in many program offerings. Other emerging factors with relatedness to program are (1) the upward revision of require-ments for admission to colleges; (2) the nature and emphases in examinations such as the College Entrance Board Examinations, Merit Board Examinations, various scholarship examinations, and the like; and (3) the intensified interest on the part of many parents and students in making early plans and preparations for college entrance, often beginning in the junior high school.

All things considered, including emerging ideas on programs for noncollege and college-bound youths and the implications for future decision making on the part of educational administrations are indeed exciting and challenging.

New Dimensions

In this precarious realm of prediction, three dimensions are emphasized: the rate and nature of educational change, educational program development, and staffing. The last two are not independent of the first, of course, but the program and staffing developments which will emerge in response to rapid educational change will be so dramatic in terms of their impact on the role of the administrator that in the paragraphs below they will be discussed separately.

Educational change. The introductory section of this chapter included the statement: "School systems have long been relatively unresponsive institutions to needed reform and change." This generalization oversimplifies a complex issue. In one respect the schools of the country might be credited with having been quite responsive to societal needs. They have expanded from nineteenth century institutions devoted largely to the college preparatory training of "the rich, the well-born, and the able" to twentieth century institutions dedicated to the education of all children for a variety of purposes. As society has requested an expansion of school services for more facets of the student's well-being (such as guidance and health and psychological services), the schools have accepted these responsibilities.

On the other hand, the basic structure of education has been resistant to change. The role of the teacher has changed little in the last century. The schoolroom with 30 children and a teacher has persisted as the basic unit of formal education. The textbook has retained its place as the center of classroom activity and the major determinant of curricular content. The manner in which the schools "weathered" the recent outburst of public interest in education following the launching of Sputnik I is a case in point. A survey of change in New York State schools following this event substantiates the distinction which is being made in the nature of school response to change:

> The study revealed that despite the number of new programs introduced, most of the accompanying changes took place *within* the existing structural framework of the schools. Schools had

tended to adopt new textbooks, alter the content of some traditional courses, add honors sections in some subjects, change the way they selected students for instructional groups, and accelerate the pace at which bright students moved through a standard sequence of courses. Few innovations embodied changes in the kind of people employed, in the way they were organized to work together, in the types of instructional materials they used, or in the times and places at which they taught. In short, *schools as structured institutions had remained stable.*[5]

It is highly likely that no such statement will be made about schools fifteen years hence. The rate of societal change, the increasing accumulation of knowledge about teaching and learning, and the burgeoning demands on the schools will inevitably cause this stable institution to become less stable. Educational administrators in the past and at the present have been characterized by (1) assuming the role of respondent to change which occurred elsewhere and (2) enjoying the luxury of making the change within the structure of a stable institutional structure. In the future, the administrator's success will depend upon (1) being able to employ the dynamics of the change process to fulfill the objectives of the school as an institution and (2) providing relative stability in an institution which is undergoing basic structural modification.

Educators should be disturbed by the minimal attention which they have paid to the process of change. The school administrator of the future will be a participant in a nationwide, organized process of change not dissimilar from that which has existed in the field of agriculture for the past half century. Federal and state governmental agencies responsible for educational coordination, research and improvement, institutions of higher education, and the public schools will become teams of professional employees working toward the improvement of education. The local school administrator will be placed in the center of this process and will spend the bulk of his time implementing the results of the process and determining its future course of action. Change will be the byword of good education, and the rigid or dogmatic administrator will have a short-lived career.

Educational program change. The nature of the change process as it is likely to affect the educational program will illustrate its new

---

[5] Henry M. Brickell, *Organizing New York State for Educational Change* (Albany, N.Y.: New York State Education Department, 1961), pp. 18–19.

dimensions. The basic question which will become the guide to administrative action is how the best learning situation can be constructed for a student with given characteristics engaged in a defined learning task or specified intellectual process. The answer to this question will not be found by studying class size or grouping students by ability. Such studies or plans are devices of administrative convenience. They begin with the assumption that there is and will continue to be a stable organizational structure of one teacher in one classroom with "n" number of students.

More sophisticated answers to the question will result in a wide diversity of structural arrangements for learning, varying from the tutorial or independent study situation to mass presentations of lectures, demonstrations, and memorization tasks. They will require instructional materials and learning devices not now available. High schools of a thousand students will have a thousand separate learning schedules for the students, not one or two basic schedules varied and repeated a thousand times. The instructional program will become what it has always been designed to be—a formal opportunity for every child to become something better than he is. At the top of this complex mechanism will be an administrator whose task it will be to exercise leadership to insure that the mechanism becomes more complex (more responsive to individual needs), while at the same time he must make it ever more simple in operating terms (that is, a mechanism which will not interfere administratively with the work and activities of the teachers and learners).

Educational staffing change.   Equally traumatic to those favoring the *status quo* will be the required changes in the area of educational staffing. New program and service dimensions will require a wide diversity of staff talents. Some staff members may be instructional programmers, while others will be consultants to individual students or to members of the teaching staff; there will also be master teachers, teacher aides, apprentice teachers, programmer teachers, student-consultant teachers, and so forth. The press of numbers of students, the multiplication of new knowledge sources, and the demand for extra services will make untenable the neat but already inadequate concept of one role for all teachers.

The divergence of staff backgrounds and assignments will affect profoundly the relationship of the administrator to the staff and general personnel administration. Specialization and advanced training by the teachers will dispel any pretense on the part of the administrator that he is a substantive expert in all the subjects and processes employed by his staff of professional workers. His relationship to the staff will become more nearly the relationship of the college administrator to his faculty. His task will be the releasing of the creative potential of this competent staff and the employment of their many talents to attain the goals of the school as an institution. He will literally not know "what is going on" in the way that today's administrator senses that he does know.

Tomorrow's school will not be "today's school but even more so." It will be an institution of quite different dimensions, sufficiently different that the change will be described as one of type rather than quantity. The same will be true of tomorrow's administrator if he is to survive as a leader and statesman playing a significant role in educational progress.

Summary

The precariousness of predicting and looking ahead in educational administration is fully acknowledged. Three levels of prognostication have been recognized in this chapter: trends, emerging developments, and calculated conjectures. Much of the material presented here has been treated in earlier chapters and no pretense of all-inclusiveness is intended. However, important highlights of trends, emerging developments, and conjectures that are likely to shape the future of educational administration are reviewed. Size factors and population, urbanization, fiscal problems, extension of services, mobility, and automation and cybernation have been cited as trends. Some emerging developments pointing to possible trends are professionalization of administrators, expansion and development of knowledge and research regarding administration, new developments and use of media, and curricular and program demands.

On the side of the conjectural (new dimensions), educational change, program innovations, and staffing considerations have been listed as among the most crucial confrontations for educational administration. Obviously, the complexity of the problems ahead in education demand unprecedented many-sided solutions.

Bibliography

American Association of School Administrators, *Educational Administration in a Changing Community*, 37th Yearbook, AASA. Washington, D.C.: AASA, 1959.

————, *In-service Education for School Administration*. Washington, D.C.: AASA, 1963.

————, *School District Organization*. Washington, D.C.: AASA, 1962.

————, *The American School Superintendency*. Washington, D.C.: AASA, 1952.

————, *Profile of The School Superintendent*. Washington, D.C.: AASA, 1960.

Association for Supervision and Curriculum Development, *Leadership for Improving Instruction*. Washington, D.C.: ASCD, 1960.

Barnard, Chester I., *The Functions of the Executive*. Cambridge, Mass.: Harvard University Press, 1938.

Bartholomew, Paul C., *Public Administration*. Paterson, N.J.: Littlefield, Adams & Co., 1959.

Brickell, Henry M., *Organizing New York State for Educational Change*. Albany, N.Y.: New York State Education Department, 1961.

Campbell, Roald F. and Russell T. Gregg, eds., *Administrative Behavior in Education*. New York: Harper & Row, Publishers, 1957.

Campbell, Roald F. and James M. Lipham, eds., *Administrative Theory as A Guide to Action*. Chicago: Midwest Administrative Center, University of Chicago, 1960.

Campbell, Roald F., John E. Corbally, Jr., and John A. Ramseyer, *Introduction to Educational Administration*. Boston: Allyn and Bacon, Inc., 1962. Chap. 11.

Coladarci, Arthur P. and Jacob W. Getzels, *The Use of Theory in Educational Administration*. Stanford, Calif.: Stanford University Press, 1955.

Conant, James B., *Slums and Suburbs*. New York: McGraw-Hill, Inc., 1961.

Corbally, John E., Jr., *School Finance*. Boston: Allyn and Bacon, Inc., 1962.

Dahlke, H. Otto, *Values in Culture and Classroom*. New York: Harper & Row, Publishers, 1958.

Ellena, William J. and Robert M. Isenberg, *School District Organization: Journey That Must Not End*. Washington, D.C.: The American Association of School Administrators, 1962.

Grieder, Calvin, Truman M. Pierce, and William Everett Rosenstengel, *Public School Administration*. New York: The Ronald Press Company, 1961. Part I.

Griffiths, Daniel E., *Administrative Theory*. New York: Appleton-Century-Crofts, Inc., 1959.

Griffiths, Daniel E., David L. Clark, D. Richard Wynn, and Laurence Iannaccone, *Organizing Schools for Effective Education*. Danville, Ill.: The Interstate Printers and Publishers, Inc., 1962. Part I.

Griffiths, Daniel E., *Research in Educational Administration: An Appraisal and a Plan*. New York: Bureau of Publications, Teachers College, Columbia University, 1959.

Halpin, Andrew W., *Administrative Theory in Education*. Chicago: Midwest Administration Center, University of Chicago, 1958.

Hemphill, John K., Daniel E. Griffiths, and Norman Frederiksen, *Administrative Performance and Personality*. New York: Bureau of Publications, Teachers College, Columbia University, 1962.

Hencley, Stephen P., and Jack A. Culbertson, eds., *Educational Research: New Perspectives*. Danville, Ill.: The Interstate Printers and Publishers, Inc., 1963.

Heyel, Carl, *Appraising Executive Performance*. New York: American Management Association, 1958.

Keppel, Francis, *Public Policy and School Administration*. Cambridge, Mass.: New School Development Council, 1961.

Knezevich, Stephen J., *Administration of Public Education*. New York: Harper & Row, Publishers, 1962. Chaps. 1, 4, 5, 6.

Knight, Douglas M., ed., *The Federal Government in Higher Education*. Englewood Cliffs, N.J.: Prentice-Hall, Inc. 1960. Chap. II.

McCloskey, Gordon, *Education and Public Understanding*. New York: Harper & Row, Publishers, 1959.

Micheal, Donald N., *Cybernation: The Silent Conquest*. Santa Barbara, Calif.: Center for the Study of Democratic Institutions, 1962.

Morphet, Edgar L., Roe L. Johns, and Theodore L. Reller, *Educational Administration—Concepts, Practices and Issues*. Englewood Cliffs, N.J.: Prentice-Hall, Inc., 1959. Part II.

National Education Association, *Financing Education for Our Changing Population*. Washington, D.C.: NEA, 1961.

National Society for the Study of Education, *Community Education: Principles and Practices from World Wide Experience*, 58th Yearbook, NSSE, Part I. Chicago, Ill.: The University of Chicago Press, 1959.

Sears, Jesse B., *The Nature of the Administrative Process*. New York: McGraw-Hill, Inc., 1950.

Simon, Herbert A., *Administrative Behavior*. New York: The Macmillan Company, 1950.

Trump, J. Lloyd and Dorsey Baynham, *Guide to Better Schools*. Chicago, Ill.: Rand McNally & Company, 1961.

Walters, J. E., *Basic Administration—The Process of Planning, Organizing, and Controlling*. Paterson, N.J.: Littlefield, Adams and Co., 1959. Part B.

Index